W9-BTR-168

CIVILIZATIONS OF THE WORLD

EXPLORING
THE LIFE, MYTH, AND ART OF
ANCIENT CHINA

EDWARD L. SHAUGHNESSY

ROSEN PUBLISHING®

New York

This edition published in 2010 by:

The Rosen Publishing Group, Inc.
29 East 21st Street
New York, NY 10010

Additional end matter copyright © 2010 by The Rosen Publishing Group, Inc.

Cover design by Matthew Cauli.

Library of Congress Cataloging-in-Publication Data

Shaughnessy, Edward L., 1952–
Exploring the life, myth, and art of ancient China / Edward L. Shaughnessy.
  p. cm.—(Civilizations of the world)
Includes bibliographical references and index.
ISBN-13: 978-1-4358-5617-2 (library binding)
1. China—Social life and customs—Juvenile literature. 2. Mythology, Chinese—Juvenile literature. 3. China—Religion—Juvenile literature. 4. Arts—China—Juvenile literature.
5. China—Intellectual life—Juvenile literature. 6. China—Civilization—Juvenile literature.
I. Title.
DS721.S4466 2010
931—dc22

                                                              2009010290

Manufactured in Malaysia

CPSIA Compliance Information: Batch #BR902021YA: For Further Information contact Rosen Publishing, New York, New York at 1-800-237-9932

CONTENTS

IMAGE AND IMAGINATION

an Feizi, an early adviser to the future First Emperor of the Qin dynasty and a source of fascinating information concerning antiquity, was once discussing a word in the classic Daoist text the *Laozi*. He noted that in Chinese the word *xiang* 象 originally meant "elephant," but over time had also come to mean "image" or "imagination." People rarely see a live elephant (*xiang*), he explained, but when they find a dead elephant's bones they draw a picture to imagine (*xiang*) its life. And that is why the word "ele-phant" has been used to describe the human imagination.

In many ways, ancient China is similar to the elephant giving up its bones—its magnificent offerings of pottery, jade, bronze, stone, bamboo, and silk permit us to imagine the ways of its life.

BELOW A beautiful ivory goblet with turquoise inlay, ca. 1200 BCE. The ancient vessel was found in Xiaotun, near Anyang, Henan province, in the tomb of Lady Hao, one of the consorts of the Shang-dynasty king Wu Ding (see pages 23, 50–51).

THE MIRROR OF HISTORY

Such is the extent of China's vast historical legacy that as early as the time of the great sage Confucius (551–479 BCE, see page 55), people were already looking back on an ancient tradition. Although Confucius changed his country in ways that he himself would never know, he claimed not to be an innovator: "I transmit but do not create. I am faithful to and delight in antiquity." Four hundred years later, Sima Qian (145–ca. 86 BCE) compiled his famous *Records of the Historian*, which narrates Chinese history from the Three August Emperors of mythological times down to the high point of the Han dynasty (Sima Qian's own era). This text was but the first in a series of dynastic histories that trace China's story through to the modern age.

China's historians were able to draw on an extensive written tradition. Long before Sima Qian's time, various writings from the beginning of the first millennium BCE were compiled into texts that became China's classics. Three in particular, the *Classic of Changes*, the *Classic of Documents*, and the *Classic of Poetry*, were read by all who could read and quoted by all who could write. By the age of Confucius, scribes remained in constant attendance upon rulers, some recording their every word and others their every action.

The scholars of ancient China were always attracted to the task of rewriting— and of writing anew—the existing historical texts. By the end of the first millennium CE, when another historian named Sima, Sima Guang (1019–1086), penned the *Comprehensive Mirror for Aid in Government* (a comprehensive history of China from the beginning of the Warring States period [480 BCE] until the end of the Tang dynasty [907 CE]), China had probably produced more books than all of the world's other civilizations combined. For better and for worse, those books are the inevitable starting point for all that we know about China's antiquity.

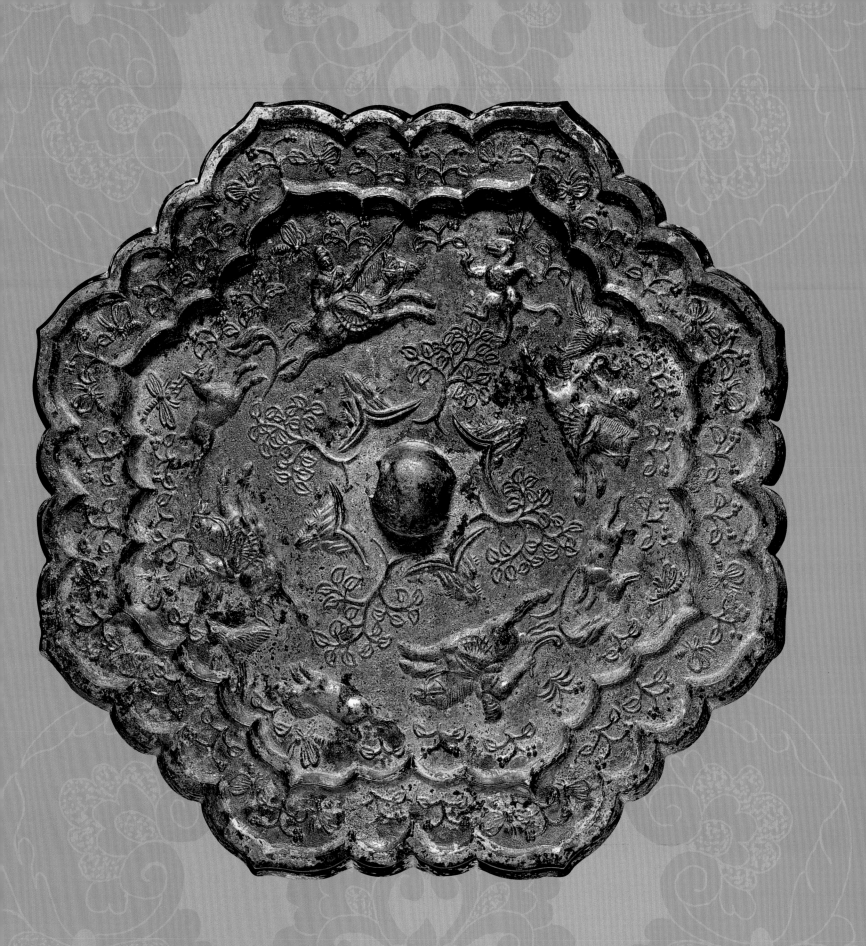

PATTERNS OF THE BIRDTRACKS

Perhaps nothing is more characteristic of China than its way of writing. Traditions credit—or rather, blame—the invention of writing on one Cangjie, a minister at the court of the legendary Yellow Emperor: "When first Cangjie observed the patterns of the birdtracks and then created writing, deceit and artifice sprouted to life." While deceit and artifice arose from the hearts of humans, writing itself is believed to have come from nature—and birdtracks were thought to constitute a natural script. Even today it is often supposed that Chinese calligraphy is natural, made up primarily of pictographs.

Although this was doubtless true of the earliest stages of the script, by the time there is actual evidence of writing (the oracle-bone inscriptions of the Shang dynasty [ca. 1200 BCE]—see photograph, left), the text was already far more complicated. It still included pictographs, such as ⊖ and 𝔻 for "sun" and "moon," or 𣂁 for "to cut a head off with an axe." There were ideographs for more abstract notions such as ⚌ for "above" (the short horizontal stroke being above the horizon), or ⽊ for "root" (the horizontal stroke indicating the

LEFT One of the many oracle bones (ca. 1200 BCE) that have been discovered at Anyang, the last capital of the Shang dynasty (see page 10), these inscribed items provide the earliest evidence of Chinese script. Chinese characters originated from simple pictographs, direct imitations of objects in the natural world, but even by the time of this oracle bone (ca. 1200 BCE) the script had already begun to evolve into the square characters of modern Chinese. This particular inscription is a divination about sending an officer by the name of Shi on an inspection, with an after-the-fact record that Shi had died twenty-eight days later.

intended place on the pictograph of a tree) and other complex graphs made up of simpler components, such as ⊖𝒟—a combination of ⊖ and 𝒟—for the concept of "brightness," or 㭧 for "forest" (three trees clustered together). But already at this time, these pictographs and ideographs were outnumbered by another category of graphs that combined one component that indicated the general classification of meaning and another component that indicated only the pronunciation. The graph 工, for example, said to be the pictograph of a carpenter's square, represented a word pronounced something like "gong" and meaning "work." When combined with 攴, which is the pictograph of a hand holding a stick, it formed the word *gong* 攻, "to attack"; with 貝, the pictograph of a cowry-shell (used in ancient China as a form of money), the word *gong* 貢, "tribute"; with ∩, the pictograph of a roof, the word *kong* 空, "empty"; with 鳥, the pictograph of a bird, the word *hong* 鴻, "goose"; and when combined with 糸, the pictograph of silk threads, it formed the word *hong* 紅, "red." The potential number of such combinations is vast, and it is this feature that has allowed the script to expand to describe the diversity of man and nature.

Over the centuries, as the script gradually evolved and as the role of pictographs became less significant and scribes required simpler forms to write, Chinese characters became ever further removed from their pictographic origins. For most people today, it would be hard to see the moon represented in the character 月, much less to see an elephant in the character 象.

ABOVE **View of a Western Zhou dynasty (ca. 1045–771 BCE) bronze *gui* grain vessel, unearthed from Famen temple in Fufeng, Shaanxi, revealing the Chinese script cast on the inside. The profusion of such inscribed antiquities has enabled scholars to gain a greater understanding of the evolution of writing in China.**

RECORDING CHINA'S STORY

RIGHT A stele from the famous Forest of Steles in Xi'an, Shaanxi, the richest, oldest, and most extensive collection of stone tablets in China, some dating back to the Han dynasty. The most effective way of ensuring the survival of important writings in ancient China was to carve them on stone—as in the case of the bold attempt to perpetuate the complete text of the Chinese classics. This first took place in 175–183 CE during the Han dynasty and then again in 241 CE during the Wei dynasty. The steles, which were erected at present-day Luoyang, were destroyed when the capital was sacked in the 4th century. Engraved again in 831–837 CE during the Kaicheng period of the Tang dynasty, the Kaicheng Stone Classics, as they are known, have survived to the present and are now housed in the Forest of Steles in Xi'an.

It was not until the end of the nineteenth century that China's earliest writings were discovered. They took the form of records of divinations performed on behalf of the last kings of the Shang dynasty (ca. 1200 BCE onward). In the West these records are known as "oracle-bone inscriptions" and in China as "shell and bone writings," since they were engraved on turtle-shell or ox bone. Public concerns such as war, flood, and famine were frequent topics of divination, but so too were more personal subjects, such as royal toothaches and the birth of heirs.

Also around this time, recipients of royal favor began to record the circumstances of their awards on bronze vessels. When the Shang dynasty was overthrown by the Zhou (1045–256 BCE), this fashion expanded dramatically, not only in terms of the number of bronzes cast but also in the actual length of the inscriptions—some reached as much as several hundred characters in extent, and provide invaluable insight into many fascinating aspects of life in the early first millennium BCE, including even the very first attempts to write history.

Although bone and bronze continued to be inscribed even in much later times, by the time of the Qin dynasty (221–207 BCE), stone had become a favored medium. After uniting China, the First Emperor of Qin had seven large stone slabs erected at prominent places throughout the empire inscribed with lengthy texts extolling his accomplishments. Others soon followed his lead, inscribing steles with everything from the classics to eulogies for deceased parents.

RIGHT This ancient wooden slip (268 CE) from Loulan, Gansu is inscribed with a letter of apology. Loulan was a military outpost established along the Han-dynasty defense lines in the desert of Central Asia. Thousands of wooden slips from the administration of the garrison there have been preserved by the arid conditions. Even in central China, where conditions for the preservation of wood have not been so favorable, there have been many notable finds in tombs in recent years. For example, 4,947 bamboo slips, many bearing portions of early military manuals, were unearthed in 1972 at Yinqueshan, Shandong.

Bronze and stone are ideal media for inscriptions intended to last in perpetuity, but not so convenient for the transmission of everyday information. There is evidence as early as the oracle-bone inscriptions of the Shang dynasty that government records were also being written on bamboo or wooden strips. Because bamboo and wood decay under most conditions, the earliest such examples discovered to date come from the tomb of the ruler of the small state of Zeng, who died in 433 BCE. However, several more discoveries in the last decade or two have provided far greater evidence for the existence of books in ancient China.

Bamboo was an excellent material for writing short texts. A strip could be cut to any desired length, and each strip would usually bear one line of writing. Multiple strips would be bound together by passing a strap of silk or leather over and through the strips, fan style; they would then be rolled into bundles. Recent discoveries of bamboo books have included philosophical texts, such as the *Classic of Changes* and the *Laozi*. Numerous other types of documents have also been unearthed—legal texts, divinations, and inventories of goods placed in tombs.

Among its other advantages, bamboo was readily available and the strips could be reused by simply shaving off the outer layer of writing. Yet even this medium was cumbersome, being heavy and clumsy to transport—many stories tell of itinerant philosophers traveling laden down with cartloads of such books. Wealthy patrons employed rolls of silk to make fair copies of their most important texts. But since silk was prohibitively expensive, the quest to develop an inexpensive substitute that would match its convenience led, by the second century CE under the Eastern Han dynasty (25–220 CE), to the invention of paper—one of China's greatest contributions to world civilization.

UNLOCKING THE UNIVERSE

The Chinese universe was traditionally believed to contain three realms, those of heaven, Earth, and humankind. During the Han dynasty (202 BCE–220 CE), philosophers portrayed the king (*wang* 王) as the agent responsible for connecting these three (三) realms and was regarded as the living link between them.

Heaven was the vault of the sky, the field upon which the sun and moon, stars and planets made their regular—and sometimes apparently irregular—movements. And, as in all early civilizations, the Chinese were keen watchers of the night sky. The five visible planets (Mercury, Venus, Mars, Jupiter, Saturn) all had their own personalities, and their effects on persons and events on Earth. The "Grand White," or Venus, far from being a goddess of love, was a baleful executioner (white being the color of mourning in China), while Saturn moved slowly like an old man and was associated with the Yellow Emperor of high antiquity. But it was the "Year

BELOW A detail from a Tang-dynasty (618–907 CE) star map, from Dunhuang, Gansu province, depicting the night sky as seen from the northern hemisphere. The complete scroll is divided into 12 sections (4 of which are shown here), which correspond to the stations of Jupiter, considered by the ancient Chinese to be the most important planet.

RIGHT An Eastern Zhou-
dynasty jade dragon
pendant, ca. 500 BCE. The
dragon was one of four
"spiritual animals"
associated with the
constellations. The mythical
creature was a symbol of
the east, springtime,
fertility, and the generative
rhythms of the elements—
its movements were
believed to correspond
exactly to the agricultural
cycle and to the seasonal
waxing and waning of the
creative *yang* principle.

Star," Jupiter, that was considered the most important
of the planets, governing time as it appeared to pass
from one constellation to another.

As elsewhere, stars were grouped into constellations: four "spiritual animals" and twenty-eight lunar
lodges being the most important of them. The celestial
"Dragon" was composed of stars from Virgo through Scorpio, and included the lodges "Horns," "Gullet," "Chest,"
"Shoulders," "Heart" (which included Antares, in China the "Fire
Star"), and "Tail" (coinciding to a great extent with the constellation
known in the West as Scorpio). At one time, its rise in the east indicated the onset of spring and the beginning of the growing season. The
dragon, embodiment of the generative force of *yang*, leaped from the
subterranean waters in which it had been trapped during the winter and
began its ascent into the night sky. By the middle of summer, when the life
forces were at their peak, its entire body would be arrayed for all to see.

If the Dragon was the constellation of the east and spring, and thus of the color
green, summer was the time of the Phoenix, red in color and associated with the
south. Winter, on the other hand, was the time of the black Turtle, which lived in
the watery abyss of the north. This explains in large part why early Chinese maps
were oriented with south at the top; water should of course be at the bottom, with
the Phoenix flying above. It begins to explain, as well, the underpinnings of the
subsequent notion of the *wu xing* or "Five Motions" or "Five Phases," of which all
matter was thought to be composed.

THE HEAVENLY DRAGON

The dragon is one of China's most ancient and potent symbols, the embodiment of vigor and strength. In summer it flies through the heavens and in winter resides in the subterranean waters. Far from a fire-breathing monster, the Chinese dragon is a benevolent creature—the supreme symbol of the emperor—that visits Earth only occasionally in response to human needs. Examples of its varied representation in Chinese art are shown in these jade plaques (opposite page, and left and right) and in a bronze musical-instrument stand (above), all from the Zhou period.

CHINA AND ITS PEOPLE

China is continental in every respect of the word, encompassing most of the East Asian landmass and including almost every climatic and topographical feature that one would expect. But while present-day China stretches from the deserts of Central Asia to the grasslands of Mongolia, and from the towering Himalayas to the tropical island of Hainan in the south, the China of antiquity is usually thought to have been cradled in the elbow of the Yellow river (see pages 32–33).

Beginning in the Kunlun Mountains of Xinjiang and Qinghai provinces, the Yellow river washes through the grainy soil of Ningxia and Mongolia, then turns due

LEFT The *ding*, or cauldron, was a cooking pot for meat, but it also had much greater significance within the symbolic world of ancient China. The *ding* was one of the most important ritual vessels in ancestral temples—for example, the ranks of the nobility were denominated by the number of them that they were allowed to display. The king was entitled to nine, symbolizing his authority over China's nine regions. This bronze vessel dates from the end of the Warring States period (480–222 BCE).

south to divide the provinces of Shaanxi and Shanxi before
hitting the stone fastness of the Qinling Mountains, which
redirect it eastward to the sea. The area "inside the river,"
or to the north and east of its great bend, is where the Xia
(ca. 2000–1550 BCE) and Shang (ca. 1550–1045 BCE)
dynasties took root, and where the subsequent "Zhong
Guo" or Central Kingdoms were located. This area is in turn
cleaved by the Taihang mountain range, stretching from Beijing in the
north to south of the river; these mountains divided the Central Kingdoms into those east of the mountains (Shandong) and those west of the
mountains (Shanxi). Throughout much of antiquity, China's primary axis was
east–west; thus we have the Western Zhou and Eastern Zhou, Western Han and
Eastern Han dynasties, and even as late as the Tang dynasty the two capitals were in
the west (at present-day Xi'an) and east (at Luoyang), respectively.

However, by the time of the Zhou dynasty, if not before, southern states along
China's other great river, the Yangzi or Long river, began to provide a counterweight
to the classical civilizations of the north. In time, the lush foliage and long growing
seasons of the south would attract more and more people to resettle there, and
by the end of antiquity the weight of these demographic changes had re-oriented
Chinese civilization. No longer would the divide be between east and west; thereafter, China's divisions would be north and south.

Within these regions there were numerous local variations. According to
legends, Yu the Great, founder of the Xia dynasty (see pages 31–34), divided China
into nine regions, each possessing distinct physical and cultural characteristics.

But who exactly were the ancient Chinese people? A generation or two ago, it was thought that archaeology would provide the answer to this question. The oldest civilizations in China seemed to be the Yangshao and Longshan neolithic cultures located in the western and eastern stretches of the Yellow river valley. According to the then prevailing theory of historical development, Chinese civilization radiated out from this one bi-polar source. Today, however, it is commonly accepted that Chinese civilization had multiple origins, with numerous local cultures coexisting, at times in contact with other cultures, at times perhaps isolated; some coming for a while to have predominance over others, some being extinguished, almost without a trace.

This theory of multiple origins was already becoming influential during the 1970s due to numerous neolithic cultures discovered throughout southern China. By 1985, when the highly developed bronze culture of Sanxingdui was unearthed near Chengdu, Sichuan, there could no longer be any doubt that different centers of civilization coexisted. The Sanxingdui culture (see photograph, page 23) created bronze artifacts the equal of any in the world, but which seem to owe little to the contemporary Shang culture, the heart of which was located far away in the northeast at Anyang. In later times, too, archaeology is revealing a persistent tension between general and local characteristics. In the Warring States period (480–222 BCE), some of the most exquisite artifacts have been discovered in what were traditionally regarded as the "barbarian" states of Zhongshan and Chu. Perhaps surprisingly, the elites of these states appear to have subscribed in large measure to the standards of civilization associated with the contemporary Zhou states. And in later periods, too, "barbarians" continued to contribute to what we now know as China.

RIGHT **This map shows China, its provinces (SHANXI, in capital letters) and autonomous regions (*QINGHAI*, in italic capital letters), together with important topographical features and places, both modern and ancient. Inset are details showing the territorial extent of three of the historical dynasties: in chronological order, from top to bottom, Zhou, Han, and Tang.**

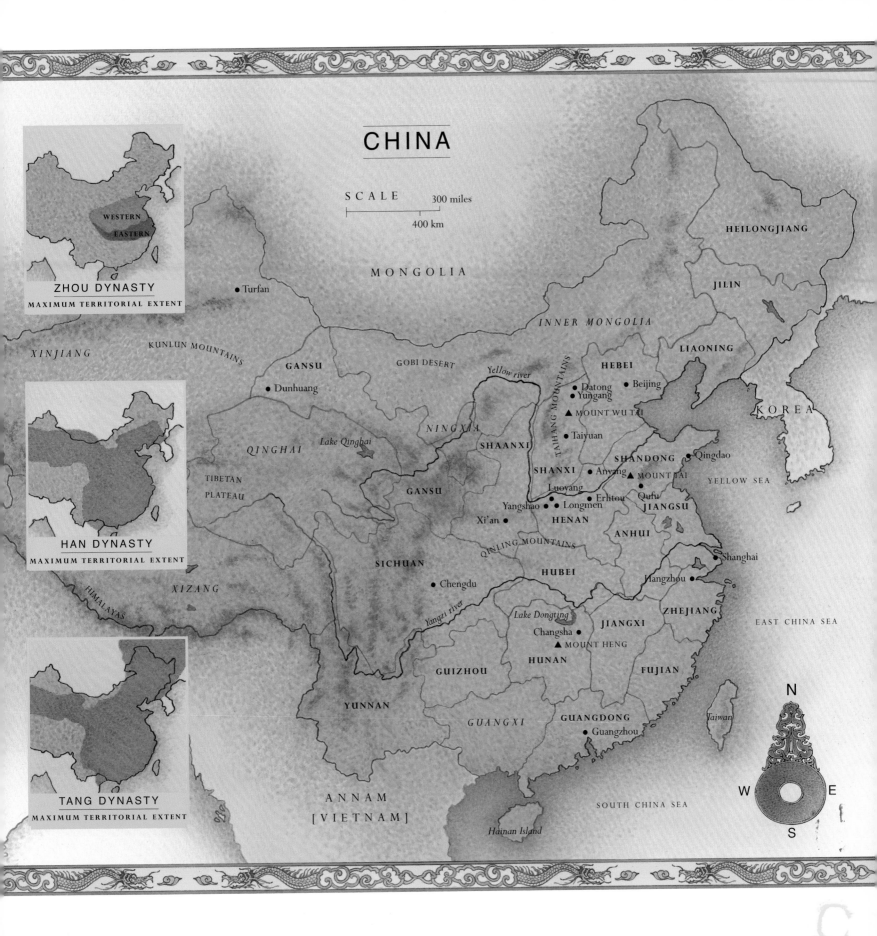

CHINA

SCALE

300 miles

400 km

ZHOU DYNASTY
MAXIMUM TERRITORIAL EXTENT

WESTERN

EASTERN

HAN DYNASTY
MAXIMUM TERRITORIAL EXTENT

TANG DYNASTY
MAXIMUM TERRITORIAL EXTENT

MONGOLIA

HEILONGJIANG

INNER MONGOLIA

JILIN

XINJIANG

KUNLUN MOUNTAINS

GANSU

GOBI DESERT

Yellow river

LIAONING

HEBEI

• Turfan

• Dunhuang

• Datong   • Beijing

• Yungang

KOREA

QINGHAI

Lake Qinghai

NINGXIA

▲ MOUNT WU TAI

SHAANXI

• Taiyuan

TAIHANG MOUNTAINS

TIBETAN

PLATEAU

GANSU

SHANXI

SHANDONG   • Qingdao

• Anyang   ▲ MOUNT TAI

YELLOW SEA

Luoyang

Yangshao • Longmen

• Erlitou

• Qufu

HIMALAYAS

XIZANG

Xi'an •

HENAN

JIANGSU

QINLING MOUNTAINS

ANHUI

SICHUAN

HUBEI

• Shanghai

• Chengdu

Yangzi river

Hangzhou •

ZHEJIANG

EAST CHINA SEA

Lake Dongting

JIANGXI

Changsha •

▲ MOUNT HENG

GUIZHOU

HUNAN

FUJIAN

Taiwan

YUNNAN

GUANGXI

GUANGDONG

N

• Guangzhou

ANNAM

[VIETNAM]

SOUTH CHINA SEA

W   E

Hainan Island

S

TREASURES OF THE EARTH

It is often said that China boasts the world's longest continuous civilization, and it is certainly the case that ancestors of the Chinese people were living in settled communities in the area now known as China no later than about 5000 BCE. Over the millennia, one historical stratum after another has accumulated, usually burying previous strata without much trace. However, beginning in antiquity, previous strata were periodically exposed, either by such human activity as construction or by natural disasters such as floods. As early as the third century BCE, unearthed elephant bones led people to imagine the shape of living elephants (see page 5).

RIGHT Han-dynasty terracotta figurines unearthed from a tomb at Mount Wei, Zhangqiu, Shandong. These figures, frozen in time, were doubtless intended to serve as escorts on the deceased's journey to the afterlife. Other significant finds from this site included pottery horses and chariots—not as grand as the terracotta army found near the tomb of the First Emperor of Qin, but still remarkable for the tomb of a local aristocrat.

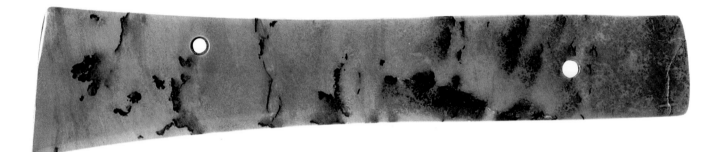

About a century thereafter, toward the end of the second century BCE, there came notable discoveries of civilization: an ancient bronze vessel unearthed in 116 BCE caused the emperor to declare a new reign era, the reign of the "Prime Cauldron;" and about the same time, workers renovating Confucius's family home found ancient books, written on bamboo strips, concealed in the walls. The official histories of the following centuries record numerous other discoveries, often included in their chapters on "auspicious portents." By the Song dynasty (960–1279), scholars began the systematic study of these ancient artifacts; the *Kao gu tu* or *Illustrations Examining Antiquity* by Lü Dalin (1046–1092) is one such work that provides not only information on where 224 ancient bronzes and jades were discovered and/or then housed, but also gives drawings and detailed measurements of them. From this developed an indigenous tradition of archaeology, called in Chinese *Kaogu xue* or "the study of examining antiquity."

The final years of the Qing (1644–1912), the last of imperial China's dynasties, saw two great discoveries that would profoundly change the status of archaeology in the country. First, in 1899, a scholar named Wang Yirong (1840–1900) recognized archaic characters on "dragon bones" that he was using to try to cure a bout of

ABOVE A jade blade, dated to the early Shang dynasty (ca. 1550–1045 BCE). Strongly identified with such virtues as courage, purity, justice, and harmony, jade was a treasured stone of the ancient Chinese (see pages 102–103). Jade is a generic term for a variety of fine stones ranging from nephrite (true jade), one of the hardest of all stones, to the more common jadeite. There are few sources of nephrite in central China and most of the jade used in ancient times seems to have come from the Kunlun Mountains in the far west of the country, the abode of the Queen Mother of the West (see page 40).

ABOVE One of the most important symbols of political and spiritual power in ancient China was the flat disc known as the *bi*. Crafted from jade or other precious materials, it was often placed in tombs on the bodies of deceased aristocrats. The jade *bi* disc shown here is dated to around 2500 to 2000 BCE.

malaria. When the source of these bones was traced to Anyang, Henan, the last capital of the Shang dynasty (ca. 1550–1045 BCE), the characters were shown to be the earliest form of writing in China. This led to the archaeological exploration of Anyang, and indeed to the further development of archaeology in China. The year after Wang Yirong's discovery, a Daoist priest also named Wang renovating Buddhist caves at Dunhuang discovered in one of them a secret chamber containing more than 10,000 manuscripts written between the fifth and tenth centuries (see page 70). Many of these were bought by Aurel Stein (1862–1943) and Paul Pelliot (1879–1945) and are now stored in the British Library in London and the Bibliothèque Nationale in Paris. These two discoveries of textual material stirred the imagination of people both in and outside of China and placed archaeology at the forefront of China's examination of antiquity.

In the early 1970s, after several decades marred by foreign aggression, civil war, and then internal turmoil, the development of Chinese archaeology reached new levels. In a very short period there were three remarkable discoveries that attracted the world's attention. In 1972 and 1973, three tombs were excavated at a site called Mawangdui, in the heart of the modern city of Changsha, Hunan. The tombs belonged to Li Cang, lord of the local kingdom of Dai (died 186 BCE), his wife (date of death

RIGHT **This extraordinary bronze statue, ca. 1200 BCE, some 6ft (1.8m) in height, was excavated from Sanxingdui, near Chengdu, Sichuan. Hundreds of bronze, stone and jade implements, gold objects, and elephant tusks, were unearthed from this site, giving archaeologists the first indication of a highly developed bronze culture far removed from the home of China's traditional dynasties (see page 18).**

unknown), and one of their sons (died 168 BCE). In Lady Dai's tomb was found her almost perfectly preserved body, while in the tomb of the son was found an extensive library of texts, many written on silk. In the next year, 1974, farmers cultivating a field near the tomb of Qin Shi Huangdi, the First Emperor (see page 58), just outside Xi'an, Shaanxi, unearthed an underground army of terracotta warriors designed to protect the First Emperor in the afterlife. Then, a year later, in Anyang, archaeologists excavated the undisturbed tomb of Lady Hao (see pages 5 and 79), one of the consorts of the Shang king Wu Ding and a figure already known from numerous oracle-bone inscriptions about her.

These discoveries, so startling at the time, have proved to be just the tip of the iceberg. Virtually each of the last thirty years has brought with it more and more remarkable excavations: pottery and jade from neolithic sites throughout central China as well as from such peripheral areas as Liangzhu in the southeast and Hong-shan in the northeast; numerous stunning bronzes, including the earliest ever found—at Yanshi Erlitou, near Luoyang, Henan, the extraordinary set of sixty-four bells from the tomb of Lord Yi of Zeng (died 433 BCE), the exotic statues and masks from Sanxingdui (see photograph, right), as well as countless bronzes from more traditional sites such as Xingan in Jiangsu, Zhouyuan in Shaanxi, Sanmenxia in Henan, and Tianma Qucun in Shanxi; lacquerware from tombs throughout southern China; so many more texts written on bamboo strips as to require a new field of study; and exquisite murals on the walls of Tang-dynasty tombs across northern China. In all, a spectacular array of magnificent artifacts made and used by the people of ancient China and which can now comple-ment the written record to help us see who they were.

MYTHS
AND BELIEFS

In China, most myths are preserved for us in the works of philosophers. Humankind's fall from a primordial golden age is narrated in the Daoist text the *Zhuangzi*. It tells how Jet-black and Blur, emperors of the north and south seas, occasionally met in the land belonging to Dumpling. Wishing to repay his kindness, they said: "All men have seven openings to see, hear, eat and breathe. He alone doesn't have these. Let's try to bore him." Each day they bored one hole. On the seventh day, Dumpling died. This story illustrates two important features of Chinese myths and religious beliefs: that the universe, like Dumpling, is a self-contained entity, with no transcendental godhead outside of it; and that for Daoism and Buddhism, desire is the root of misfortune.

THE MAKING OF THE WORLD

Classical Chinese philosophical sources describe the origins of the world as a state without differentiations: no light, no dark; no high, no low. Empty yet full, all matter was combined in a moist, dumpling-like sac. According to one source, out of this undifferentiated state, called Tai Yi or Grand Unity, water was born. The mixture of this water with Grand Unity then gave forth heaven, which in turn joined with Grand Unity to produce Earth. Heaven and Earth then united to give birth to the spirits and the luminaries, who gave birth to the *yin* and *yang* (see page 78), which in turn produced the four seasons. From these came hot and cold, which produced moist and dry, which is to say the year, which is to say time, which is the culmination of evolution.

Humankind is noticeably absent from this account of the world's beginnings. Mythology provides two different explanations for the creation of humankind—one from a man and one from a woman. The man, apparently, was one Pan Gu, "Coiled Antiquity," the personification of Grand Unity. When nearing death, his body exploded: his breath became the wind, his left eye the sun, his right eye the moon, his four limbs the four quarters of the world, his blood its rivers and seas, and so on. The lice on his skin were touched by the wind, and these became people. Another tradition credits a woman, Nü Wa, as the creator of humankind. One telling says that she used the clay of the earth to make people—the noble ones yellow, the meaner ones darker. Another says that she joined with her brother, Fuxi, the only other person alive, and together they made children.

The progenitors of the world were busy fighting. Many myths tell of battles between the gods, which seem to have resulted in the differentiation of time. Perhaps best known is the battle between Chi You, a reptilian monster, and Huang

Di, the Yellow Emperor. At the beginning of the battle, Chi You, the Yellow Emperor's minister in charge of the waters, caused a great fog to descend, blurring everything. To find his bearings, the Yellow Emperor invented the south-pointing chariot, or the compass. Finally, he sent the daughter of heaven, Ba, or Drought, to dry out the fog, and then he killed Chi You. At this, Chi You transformed into a comet—an inconstant star. In later times, his reappearances foreboded warfare.

Another version of this myth concerns Gong Gong, ruler of a flooded earth prior to the time of the Yellow Emperor. After being deposed, the enraged Gong Gong butted his head against Buzhou Shan, the Incomplete Mountain, in the western Kunlun Mountain range. When this pillar of heaven collapsed, heaven tilted down in the west while the earth tilted up—this is why the stars appear to move across the skies from east to west, and why the rivers of China flow from west to east.

Not all chaos is caused by water—an abundance of suns can be equally disruptive. In later antiquity, ten suns appeared at once (doubtless the reason the Chinese traditionally divided time into ten-day weeks). The people were saved by the archer Yi, who shot nine of them out of the sky. Many other Chinese myths are set in the night sky.

RIGHT **A 7th-century Chinese silk funerary banner depicting Nü Wa and her brother/husband, Fuxi—considered by some sources to be the progenitors of the Chinese people—entwined in cosmic harmony. Their wings are a symbol of immortality.**

The feuding brothers Shishen and Yanbo, gods of the Xia and Shang peoples, could not stand to be in each other's sight. Their father, the emperor Gao Xin, therefore banished them to the sky where they now appear as stars within Orion and the Pleiades; one rises in the east as the other sets in the west. Even better known is the story of the mortal Herdboy and the divine Spinning Girl—represented by the stars Vega and Altair—whose romance offended the heavenly authorities. They were sentenced to meet only once a year, the seventh day of the seventh month, when a bridge of magpies forms over the Han river—the Milky Way. The dragon, the symbol of the sage and emperor (see page 14), makes its only appearances in the night sky.

Even Tai Yi or Grand Unity was an astral deity. It referred to the topmost of a group of four stars in an inverted Y-shape located just above the northern Dipper, and seems to have governed military campaigns, as demonstrated by its use in decorating the blade of a dagger-axe from the Warring States period. By 112 BCE, Emperor Wu of Han (reigned 141–87 BCE) had established two different altars dedicated to Tai Yi to conduct the state's most important sacrifices. In the *Records of the Historian* of Sima Qian (145–ca. 86 BCE), there is the following account of a ritual performed at the outset of a military campaign in that same year: "[Emperor Wu] was about to launch an attack on Nan Yue, and offered prayers for success to Grand Unity. A banner painted with the sun, moon, the Northern Dipper, and the Ascending Dragon served as the Grand Unity spear, and was called the Numinous Flag. While performing the prayer for success in battle, the Grand Scribe raised the flag and pointed it at the country to be attacked." A similar banner to the one described in this ritual was discovered in a tomb dating to 168 BCE at Mawangdui, in Changsha, Hunan. It is a painting on silk that is labeled "Diagram for Repelling Weapons."

BUILDERS OF CIVILIZATION

BELOW One of the most enduring cultural legacies of the ancient Chinese was the development of highly impressive techniques for rice cultivation, as shown in these magnificent rice terraces in southern China. (See also caption page 31.)

Fuxi, the brother/husband of Nü Wa, and thus the progenitor of the Chinese people (see page 26), was responsible for several important cultural inventions. By his union with Nü Wa, he of course invented marriage. The carpenter's square with which he is usually pictured indicates his role in teaching the people to work. And through careful observation of the patterns of the heavens and Earth, he created the hexagrams of the *Yi Jing* or *Classic of Changes*, and these in turn served him as models to make nets for hunting and fishing. His epoch was followed by that

of Shen Nong, the Divine Farmer, who invented the plow and also established the first market, so that people could exchange their produce. When Shen Nong died, Huang Di, the Yellow Emperor, succeeded him as the third of the Three August Emperors. He is said to have invented not only armor (to defend himself against the weapons invented by Chi You), medicine, and pottery but also the south-facing chariot—that is, the compass (see page 27).

These Three August Emperors were followed by the Five Emperors of antiquity: Zhuan Xu, Di Ku, Yao, Shun, and Yu, who collectively institutionalized government. The last of these Five Emperors, Yu (often known as Yu the Great), earned the position of emperor by saving the people from a catastrophic flood that completely covered China. After draining the waters into the sea, he divided the land into nine different regions and established taxes that each region submitted to the central state. He also cast nine bronze cauldrons, each depicting the monsters of the various regions, so that the people living there could recognize them and be protected from them. The "Nine Regions" has since become a standard name for the land of China, and throughout antiquity the nine cauldrons were thought to symbolize authority over it. Yu's accomplishments in hydrology and metallurgy would have guaranteed his fame, even if he had not also established dynastic rule by being the first of the ancient emperors to pass power on to his own son, Qi, who is said to have created the Xia dynasty, the first of China's traditional dynasties (see page 34).

ABOVE **A large, Six Dynasties period (222–589 CE) earthenware model of a cart with a bull and human figures. According to legend, Shen Nong, the Divine Farmer, invented the plow, thus leading the Chinese people away from hunting and fishing toward farming and the development of a more sophisticated agrarian culture. Such mastery of the natural environment of course proved to have a dramatic impact on Chinese life and civilization.**

THE YELLOW RIVER

The Yellow river (see photograph, right) is the cradle of China's civilization, the territory of the Three Dynasties of China's high antiquity—the Xia, Shang, and Zhou—all of which extended along both sides of some part of the river's course.

Beginning in the Kunlun Mountains of Chinese Central Asia, the Yellow river flows some 3,395 miles (5,464 km) before emptying into the Bay of Bohai, draining almost the entirety of northern China. Much of the area through which it flows is made up of a very fine particulate soil, usually referred to as loess, that the river carries with it. It is this sediment—as much as 2.3 lbs per cubic foot (37 kg per cubic meter) of water—that gives the Yellow river its peculiar color, and thus its name. This sediment also has caused the river to rise, so that for the last 500 miles (800 km) of its course it actually flows, constrained within levees, as much as 33 feet (10 m) above the surrounding countryside. When it breaches the levees, as it has done repeatedly over the millennia, it usually changes its course, often quite dramatically.

The theme of flooding is very prominent in Chinese mythology. Yu the Great (see page 31) is said to have earned his eminence as emperor by having saved China from terrible floodwaters that covered it during the reigns of Yao and Shun. His father, Gun, had initially been commanded to tame the waters, but his dam-building method proved unsuccessful. Yu, however, employed a more effective strategy to control the floods—he dredged the river courses so that the waters could flow to the seas.

THE QUESTION OF XIA

According to tradition, the sage emperors Yao and then Shun were served by several eminent ministers: Yi, Gao Yao, Kui, as well as Yu the Great (see page 31). The emperor Shun named Yu as his successor. On the emperor's death, Yu attempted to turn over power to Shun's son, Shangjun, but the many lords of the world would not accept him, and forced him into exile. Thus, Yu became the emperor in his turn. When he died, his former colleague Yi was appointed to succeed him. Traditions are divided over what happened next. The earliest sources suggest that Yu's death was followed by a power struggle, with Yu's son, Qi, killing Yi and then taking power for himself. Other sources, which have become orthodox, say that Yi ruled only during the three-year mourning period for Yu, and then voluntarily yielded authority to Qi. Since Qi's kingship marked the establishment of dynastic rule in China, it can be imagined why the earlier story was suppressed.

The *Zhushu Jinian* or *Bamboo Annals* indicates that descendants of Yu ruled as the Xia dynasty for seventeen generations and 471 years. The last king of the dynasty, Jie or Di Gui, is the first of the evil last emperors who have become paradigmatic in Chinese history. Standard sources simply say that he was lacking in virtue, but others describe his sexual debauchery. All suggest that even heaven showed its displeasure: during Jie's reign, the visible planets are said to have criss-crossed (which they indeed seem to have done in 1576 BCE) and some years later, two suns appeared at the same time—apparently symbolizing the rise of a new dynasty, the Shang.

There are no written records from the time of the Xia dynasty—many therefore regard it as legendary, although others believe that there is archaeological evidence that points clearly to its existence (see caption, right). The question of Xia has thus become one of the more contentious issues in the study of ancient China.

RIGHT This bronze ornamental plaque with turquoise inlay (1700–1500 BCE), unearthed in Henan, is from the Erlitou culture, which flourished during the time of the Xia dynasty (ca. 2000–1550 BCE), believed by some to be mythical. Numerous similar bronze artifacts, as well as a vast palace, dating to around the same period, have also been discovered in the Henan and Shanxi regions (the area associated with the Xia)—many scholars consider such discoveries as undoubted proof of the existence of the dynasty. With its somewhat monstrous face and bulbous eyes, it is not known exactly what the creature shown here represents. It was found on the body of a buried man—a person of some prominence, judging by the other bronze, jade, and turquoise objects also unearthed there.

THE SYMMETRY OF *TAOTIE*

The *taotie* or animal-mask design was ancient China's most popular motif. It originated on jade pieces, such as this *cong* (above; see also page 103), among the Neolithic cultures of the eastern seaboard and was common on bronze ritual vessels of the Shang dynasty (opposite). In later times, when the animal-head handles here (ca. 250 BCE, left and right) were made, the design was associated with an "insatiable monster," but there is no contemporary evidence for this. *Taotie*'s symmetry, focused on the two eyes, was especially well adapted to ancient China's piece-mold method of casting bronze vessels. Unlike the lost-wax casting of the West, piece-mold casting allowed the artisan access to the inside of the mold, and so made possible the intricate designs found on the exterior surface of the bronze pieces.

WORTHY TO RULE

The ancient Chinese were keen observers of the night sky. They saw in the regular and, especially, the irregular movement of the sun and moon, stars and planets, expressions of heaven's will. One of the cornerstones of Chinese political philosophy is that heaven gives its mandate to rule only to a worthy recipient. But when that recipient, or his heirs, no longer merits the mandate, heaven may also take it away. In King Jie's reign, heaven was thought to have demonstrated its displeasure by causing the planets to alter their regular movement and by making

two suns appear together (see page 34). Five hundred years later, in 1059 BCE, there was another celestial omen—a spectacular conjunction of the five visible planets—and this portended that it was the turn of the Shang dynasty, the successor to the Xia, to lose its mandate. Its last ruler, King Zhou (not to be confused with the Zhou of the following Zhou dynasty), is usually twinned with King Jie—they have the reputation as the two most evil kings of antiquity. Not only did Zhou follow Jie in debauchery (he is said to have filled ponds with wine and hung meat from trees, under which he made the men and women of his court chase each other), but he even surpassed him in cruelty.

LEFT **Twilight at Mount Huang, in southern Anhui province. Observation of the skies played a key role in ancient Chinese life. Heaven, Earth, and humankind were believed to be closely linked—a change in one realm was thought to affect all others.**

The tales of Jie's and Zhou's debaucheries—told by the subsequent vanquishers of their dynasties, and thus almost certainly much exaggerated—set the tone for later rulers. In a similar vein, King You, the last king of the Western Zhou dynasty (reigned 781–771 BCE) is said to have lost his kingdom trying to please his dour consort Bao Si—a woman who rarely smiled. However, she was once amused when, on seeing that beacon fires were lit (which indicated an enemy attack), allied armies rushed to defend the capital, only to find that there was no attack at all. The king, seeking to make her laugh some more, continued this trick until the allies no longer bothered to respond to the warning beacons. Shortly thereafter, however, the capital came under a real attack, and the king was killed and the dynasty ended. In so many of these legends, women are made to bear the blame for the blunders of men.

QUEEN MOTHER OF THE WEST

Chinese mythology's antipathy toward women is such that there is no significant mother goddess similar to those found in other civilizations. However, even by the time of the Shang dynasty there is mention in the oracle-bone inscriptions of a "western mother," who may well be a goddess figure. By the fourth and third centuries BCE, the Queen Mother of the West had become a standard trope. Living in the Kunlun Mountains of the far west, she presided over a paradise of immortality. She is depicted in various guises, sometimes human, sometimes animal, sometimes a mixture of the two, and sometimes in the form of a woman riding on a tiger—in all cases, she can be identified by her distinctive headdress.

One of the earliest texts describes the travels of King Mu (Zhou dynasty; reigned 956–918 BCE) to the Kunlun Mountains. Although the king fell in love with the Queen Mother of the West, and she with him, he had to return alone to the world of men. In later centuries, men from all walks of life sought to join her in the realm of immortality. The "Record of Omens and Portents" of the *Book of Han* records that in the year corresponding to 3 BCE, there was a messianic religious movement devoted to her; the people believed that those who wore her talisman would not die. In the next two centuries, her image appeared throughout China in various forms, including in murals, and even on mirrors and bricks. By the third century, when the Daoist religion coalesced, the Queen Mother of the West was the highest ranking female divinity. Her abode in the Kunlun Mountains became the axis by which to ascend to heaven. By the Tang dynasty, when Daoism had become the state religion, shrines to her occupied central places on both Mount Tai, the sacred mountain of the east, and of course Mount Hua, the sacred mountain of the west, and many of the great poets of the age sang of her glories.

RIGHT The Queen Mother of the West (Xi Wang Mu) was one of China's most revered female deities, courted by emperors and commoners alike. A poem by Yang Xiong (53 BCE–18 CE) in praise of emperor Cheng, states: "Thinking of the Queen Mother of the West,/In a state of joy he makes offerings to obtain immortality." Such was her popularity that she was immortalized in various different forms, and is depicted here on a molded brick (Eastern Han period, 25–220 CE) excavated from a tomb in Qingbaixiang, Xindu county, Sichuan, in 1954. She is shown seated on a throne formed by a tiger and a dragon, with several male figures and various creatures in attendance, including a hare and a nine-tailed fox, all of whom bear symbolic significance.

DAOISM

Messianic groups began to appear in China toward the end of the Western Han dynasty (202 BCE–9 CE). Some of these were led by members of the Li family, which claimed descent from Li Er, more often known as Laozi, author of the *Dao De Jing* or *Classic of the Way and Virtue*. By the second century CE, these groups had coalesced into two or three mass religious movements, all of them inspired by the deified Laozi, and all of them claiming to be the *Dao* or the "Way." In 142, one Zhang Daoling, living in the southwestern province of Sichuan, claimed to have received a revelation from Laozi ordering him to establish a new religion to replace

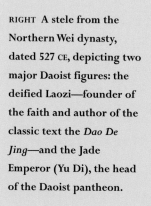

RIGHT **A stele from the Northern Wei dynasty, dated 527 CE, depicting two major Daoist figures: the deified Laozi—founder of the faith and author of the classic text the *Dao De Jing*—and the Jade Emperor (Yu Di), the head of the Daoist pantheon.**

the popular religious practices, which he claimed had degenerated into demonism. Zhang and his descendants created a religious state in Sichuan, largely independent from the Han central government, which was then in decline. The state was organized into parishes, each with its own priest or libationer. The Zhangs ruled atop an intricate hierarchy, taking the title Heavenly Masters (*tianshi*), from which the religion gets its standard name: the Way of the Heavenly Masters.

Just before the final collapse of the Han court, Zhang Lu, grandson of Zhang Daoling, collaborated with Cao Cao (155–220), the warlord of eastern China and future founder of the Wei dynasty; this earned the religion official recognition, and brought its hierarchy to the imperial capital at Luoyang. Nevertheless, elsewhere in China other variants of Daoism sprouted. Doubtless the most important developments took place in the southeast, first at Mount Mao (Maoshan), near present-day Nanjing, Jiangsu, where a man named Yang Xi received revelations from gods of the Heaven of Highest Purity (Shang Qing). These revelations persisted for six years (between 364 and 370), and Yang transcribed their instructions into a new scriptural religion, known as the Way of Highest Purity. Shortly thereafter, Ge Chaofu, scion of an illustrious southern Daoist family, composed the *Lingbao Jing* or *Classic of the Numinous Treasure*, which gave Daoism a still more elaborate theology.

State support for Daoism was strongest during the Tang dynasty, the founders of which, Li Yuan (565–635; reigned as Gaozu, 618–626) and his son Li Shimin (597–649; reigned as Taizong, 626–649), claimed descent from Li Er or Laozi. The Tang emperors were regarded as reincarnations of the historical Laozi, and candidates for government office were examined for their knowledge of the Daoist scriptures.

BUDDHISM

Originally deriving from the teachings of Gautama Siddharta throughout the Indian subcontinent in the sixth and fifth centuries BCE, Buddhism developed over the next several centuries into a sophisticated religion with numerous scriptures, known in Sanskrit as *sutra*s. Traders along the Silk Route of Central Asia brought the religion to China in the middle of the Han dynasty, a time of considerable religious ferment in the country. The earliest missionaries strove to translate the foreign Buddhist concepts into an idiom that would be both linguistically and conceptually familiar to the Chinese people. For this reason, they borrowed heavily from the language of the Daoist scriptures (in Chinese called *jing*). Over the next two or three centuries, as both Daoism and Buddhism went through numerous developments, it was unclear to many Chinese people precisely what it was that differentiated the two traditions.

Certain aspects of Buddhist theology were quite familiar to the Chinese. The earliest *sutra*s to be translated tended to deal with rules for life and techniques of meditation similar to those that were developing within the Daoist religion, and even the terminology used in the translations tended to borrow from indigenous Daoist terms.

Thus, in 166 CE, Emperor Huan of the Han dynasty performed a joint sacrifice to Laozi and to the Buddha. However, as more *sutra*s were translated (according to one count, by the eighth

BELOW Frontispiece and text from the world's oldest printed book, the Chinese translation of the Buddhist *Diamond Sutra*. Dating from 868 CE, it was discovered in the caves at Dunghuang in 1907. The book itself consists of a continuous scroll, some 16 feet (4.9 m) in length. The image shown here depicts the Buddha (center) preaching to his elderly disciple, Subhuti (bottom left).

century, as many as 1,124 had been translated into Chinese), and as the translation style became ever more rigorous, sharp differences between the two religions came into focus. Perhaps the element that was most foreign to China was the Buddhist insistence that monks should lead celibate lives—this contradicted the traditional Chinese notion that the first duty of any son was to produce a son of his own so that the ancestral lineage would be perpetuated, and it was often mentioned in nativist criticisms of the religion.

Nevertheless, the Buddhist faith exerted an enormous influence over Chinese civilization. Various dynasties, especially those headed by non-Chinese in north China during the fourth through to the sixth centuries, adopted Buddhism as the state religion and sponsored artistic projects that transformed Chinese art; Daoism assimilated much of Buddhism's elaborate description of the other world, and even Confucians accepted Buddhist methods of argumentation and metaphysics; Buddhist monasteries became hubs of commercial activity, contributing, among other things, to the development of paper currency; and the Buddhist community at Dunhuang (see page 70) preserved for us the greatest trove of medieval manuscripts—on many diverse topics and in several different languages.

ABOVE Three imposing guardians of the Buddhist faith are depicted on the limestone north wall of the Fengxian temple at the Longmen caves, near Luoyang, Henan province. The figures, from left to right, show: the *bodhisattva* (enlightenment being) Samantabhadra; the *lokapala*, or guardian of Buddhist teaching, Vaishravana; and a celestial benevolent king. The carvings are dated to 655–675 CE.

THE YUNGANG BUDDHIST CAVES

The earliest and in many ways most spectacular Buddhist cave-temples in China are those at Yungang (Cloud Ridge), just outside the city of Datong in northern Shanxi province. Called Pingcheng, this was the capital of the Northern Wei dynasty (383–534 CE), which ruled much of northern China during the period of north–south division (see pages 66–67). The Wei rulers were Toba people, of mixed Turkic and Mongol ancestry, and were great patrons of Buddhism.

In total, fifty-three out of more than 250 caves at Yungang are said to contain over 51,000 carvings. Work on the caves began in 452, the best known of which contain colossal rock-carved statues of the Buddha and the *bodhisattva* ("enlightenment being") Maitreya, which are reputed to commemorate earlier Wei rulers. The imposing seated figure shown here (right) is from Cave 13 and is more than 56 feet (17 m) high. It is believed to have been commissioned by the emperor Xiaowen in honor of his father and is considered a masterpiece of early Chinese Buddhist cave art.

The interior walls of many of the caves bear intricate carvings of scenes from Buddhist *sutra*s (sacred writings), the later of the caves showing more and more evidence of native Chinese artistic influence. All the main work on the caves was completed by 490, just before the Wei capital was moved from Pingcheng to the more centrally located Luoyang, in Henan province.

THE MANDATE OF HEAVEN

China boasts the longest unbroken history of any of the world's great civilizations, with written records dating to the Shang dynasty (ca. 1550–1045 BCE). Throughout China's ancient period, dynasties followed each other in irregular succession, some lasting for centuries but others barely outliving their founders. Already by the beginning of the Zhou dynasty (1045–256 BCE), the problem of succession had given rise to China's most important governmental principle—the Mandate of Heaven—according to which heaven confers its blessing, and thus legitimacy, only on the virtuous. If and when rulers were no longer virtuous, heaven was seen to mandate a new dynasty. From this principle developed a core notion of the dynastic cycle, wherein founding emperors were seen as strong and upright while the last ones were seen as weak and corrupt.

SHANG: THE FIRST DYNASTY

BELOW The reign of the
Shang dynasty king Wu
Ding was notable for the
development of impressive
techniques for the design
and decoration of Chinese
bronzes, as shown on this
magnificent Shang food
vessel. Such vessels were
crucial to Shang ritual
life—they were the means
by which offerings could
be made to the ancestors
and spirits, and their
ornamentation bore
symbolic significance.
(See also pages 106–107.)

The Shang or Yin dynasty (ca. 1550–1045 BCE) is China's first truly historical dynasty. The *Records of the Historian* of Sima Qian (145–ca. 86 BCE), the orthodox history of China down to about 100 BCE, provides a glowing account of Cheng Tang's defeat of King Jie of the preceding Xia dynasty (ca. 2000–1550 BCE), and a contrasting glowering account of the reign of King Zhou, the Shang dynasty's last ruler, but there is little of substance about the intervening four hundred and more years.

However, part of this story became clearer just over one hundred years ago, when oracle-bone inscriptions from the period were first recognized. Many of the tens of thousands of pieces of turtle-shell and ox-bone that have been discovered since—and certainly the majority of the most important ones—derive from the reign of King Wu Ding (reigned ca. 1200 BCE). Wu Ding appears to have inherited a state in some disarray. His uncle, King Pan Geng (reigned ca. 1250 BCE), had moved

the capital to present-day Anyang, Henan, north of the Yellow river and just east of the Taihang mountain range, apparently hoping thereby to protect the ruling house. Wu Ding managed in the course of his reign to extend Shang power not only throughout eastern China, but also west of the Taihang. This seems to have opened the Shang state to influences from the west that transformed many features of life (with, for example, the introduction of the chariot), art (see caption, left), and perhaps even myth (the native religion, centered on Di and the ancestors of the Shang kings, found itself challenged by the more catholic faith of the Zhou that featured a

heaven that embraced all peoples). Some of these innovations are apparent from the tomb of Fu Hao, one of Wu Ding's three principal consorts, which was excavated in 1975. Wu Ding's death seems to have brought about a retrenchment in Shang power back behind the natural barrier of the Taihang Mountains.

The last 150 years of the dynasty was a period of relative stagnation. Divinations performed on behalf of the kings became routine, mere expressions of hopes for a happy future; bronze vessels, although still impressive, did not develop greatly from the styles introduced during the time of Wu Ding; and military and political power seems to have become quite limited. But the Shang capital at Anyang remains perhaps the crowning glory of modern Chinese archaeology; it was the first site to be explored by the national Institute of History and Philology, the predecessor to the current Institute of Archaeology, which in its own turn has established a permanent archaeological station there.

ABOVE In the 3rd millennium BCE in the far north of China, the Hongshan culture produced delicate jade plaques in the shapes of birds and animals. Many years later these objects were to inspire artists of the Shang dynasty (ca. 1550–1045 BCE), who produced very similar jade pieces, such as this owl plaque. (See also pages 102–103.)

GOLDEN AGE OF THE ZHOU

The fall of the Shang dynasty in 1045 BCE ushered in a period that Chinese of all later ages have looked back on as a golden age of government and culture. Shang oracle-bone inscriptions reveal that the Zhou people, located in the Wei river valley of western Shaanxi province, had long been in contact with the Shang, sometimes as allies, sometimes as enemies. Their conquest campaign was planned by King Wen (reigned ca. 1099–1050 BCE)—who died before it could be carried out—and successfully concluded by King Wu (reigned 1049–1043 BCE), who was one of nine sons by King Wen's primary consort. Other sons were deputed to govern colonies and indigenous peoples throughout the eastern territories, establishing a cultural and political network that would develop into the "Central Kingdoms"— and then, eventually, into the "Central Kingdom," or China.

Many of China's cultural traditions have their roots in the portion of this dynasty known as the Western Zhou (1045–771 BCE), including the kinship system and the form of ancestor worship peculiar to it; music and poetry; the worldview that gave rise to correlative philosophy (see page 112); tax codes and legal statutes;

and, perhaps most important of all, government in which the king and his ministers ruled in an often uneasy tension. Many of these traditions seem to have developed in the middle of the 275-year-long period. Inscribed bronze vessels from this time suggest that the power of the Zhou kings began to wane; as it did so, other types of power developed. Since these other powers were in competition—with each other as well as with royal power—they required codification. In many ways, this provided the foundation for the highly developed bureaucracy of later Chinese history.

In 771 BCE, "barbarian" invaders sacked the Zhou capital near present-day Xi'an, Shaanxi, and killed King You (reigned 781–771 BCE), the last of the Western Zhou kings. King You's son, King Ping (reigned 770–720 BCE), reestablished the dynasty at its eastern capital at present-day Luoyang, Henan, but neither he nor his successors over the next five hundred years were able to reassert control over the many states of the east, nor to reclaim their traditional homeland in the west.

The Eastern Zhou period (770–256 BCE) is usually divided into two separate periods, the Spring and Autumn period (722–481 BCE) and the Warring States

BELOW An extremely rare gilt-bronze sword, dating to the Warring States period (480–222 BCE). Swords such as this developed in southeastern China, south of the Yangzi river—an area where many of China's metallurgical developments seem to have been spurred.

period (480–222 BCE). The latter name is unfortunate in associating what was in fact a dynamic period primarily with death and destruction. There were many positive developments, both technological and intellectual, that transformed the China of high antiquity. Although there was plentiful warfare, it too was influenced by and contributed to many of these developments. For instance, the invention of efficient iron plows increased food production, which contributed to a population explosion. This helped to swell the size of the armies put into the field during the period, which led to changed modes of warfare. The chariot battles of antiquity gave way to massed infantry armies, whose soldiers were equipped with the newly introduced and easily mastered crossbow. The greater number of soldiers also made discipline and logistics crucial. To meet this need, professional generals were armed with manuals detailing the art of war, the famous *Art of War of Sunzi* (*Sunzi bing fa*) being just one example of the genre. The administrative skills developed by these generals contributed, in turn, to increasingly sophisticated government administration in several of the independent states, especially Qi in the northeast, Chu in the south, and Qin in the west. Ministers in Qin created a theoretical framework for the art of government that would eventually lead to Qin's absorption of the other major states into a single grand empire, and that formed the basis of most political philosophy throughout China's imperial period.

It is, indeed, philosophy that most people associate with the Eastern Zhou period, and it is clear that it was undoubtedly an age of great intellectual ferment. It was the time

BELOW This red earthenware bowl, decorated with slip and glass (Eastern Zhou period, 770–256 BCE), is believed to have come from Xun county, Henan province.

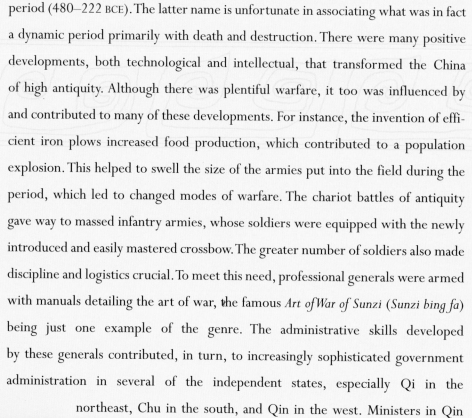

ABOVE A strand of exquisite colored glass beads from the Warring States period (480–222 BCE). Glass seems to have been introduced to China at about this time from areas to the west, in Central Asia.

of Confucius (551–479 BCE; see caption, right) and Mozi (ca. 478–392 BCE), of Laozi (ca. sixth century BCE) and Zhuangzi (ca. 365–285 BCE), of Mencius (ca. 390–305 BCE) and Xunzi (ca. 310–215 BCE), and all the other thinkers who would come to be called the "Hundred Schools." It was the time when the classics were first read and studied, and when the first real books were written. Recent archaeological discoveries of inscriptions and manuscripts from the period have revealed still more. As in the case of military and government treatises, it is clear that the period saw the rise of much technical literature—works on medicine, divination, farming, and possibly cookery, were written and circulated. This technical literature was also read by the philosophers of the day, who adapted many of its concepts for use in their own work.

LEFT **Kong Qiu or Confucius (551–479 BCE) is universally acclaimed as China's greatest sage. Although disarmingly simple, his teachings have had a global impact. His fundamental message, based on the concept of** ren **("humaneness"), was that one should act in recognition of the basic human relationships: those between parent and child, husband and wife, subject and ruler, employer and employee, and so on. Ideally, one should develop the core virtue of** ren **and strive to become emotionally centered (**zhong**) but also able to identify with others (**shu**). Confucius's favorite disciple was one Yan Hui—he was considered so important that a large temple (see left) was dedicated to him in Qufu, Confucius's place of birth.**

ANCIENT CHINESE COINS

Ancient bronze coins have been unearthed in almost all of the independent states of the Spring and Autumn and Warring States periods (722–222 BCE), their widespread distribution providing evidence that commerce thrived in ancient China. The earliest coins were made in the shapes of tools, such as shovels and knives, and denominated in quantities of silk, traditionally the most valuable commodity. Because these tool-coins proved unwieldy, they were later replaced by round coins, which could be strung together through their central hole. The examples here show a bronze shovel-coin, 8th–7th-century BCE (opposite), a knife-coin (above, center, 7 CE), and two circular coins with square holes (above, left and right, 188–618 CE).

THE FIRST EMPEROR OF QIN

Chinese historians have traditionally viewed the Qin people as unsophisticated westerners, capable only of warfare and tyrannous governmental administration. But recent archaeological discoveries suggest that this is an unfair characterization. Bronze inscriptions from the early seventh century BCE show the Qin rulers to have regarded themselves as the cultural heirs of the founding fathers of the Zhou dynasty, kings Wen and Wu, and bamboo-strip manuscripts from the third century BCE show their administrators to have been conscientious public servants—or relatively so at least. Although the state would undoubtedly have engaged in aggression and treachery against its rivals throughout the intervening five hundred or so years, this was nevertheless standard practice throughout all the states.

Histories of Qin usually focus on King Zheng of Qin, the ruler who succeeded in defeating all the other states and establishing himself as the First Emperor (reigned 221–210 BCE; the title Shi Huangdi, which he chose himself, would be better rendered as First August Theocrat, Di being the name for one of ancient China's high gods). Accounts of the era prior to the First Emperor's reign tend to do little more than contribute to idle gossip and speculation. But in the century preceding the First Emperor's reign, the state of Qin benefited from two very capable rulers: Lord Huiwen (reigned 337–311 BCE), who declared Qin to be a kingdom in 324 BCE, and King Zhao (reigned 306–251), whose fifty-five-year reign set the stage for the eventual Qin conquest. These rulers were advised by a pair of ministers, Shen Buhai (died ca. 337 BCE) and Shang Yang (died 338 BCE), who developed a political philosophy, usually referred to as Legalism, that envisioned a governmental apparatus that would be able to function on its own in an objective

and unprejudiced manner. This philosophy was subsequently brilliantly synthesized by Han Feizi (died 233 BCE), who briefly acted as a minister to the future First Emperor (see page 5).

With the final conquest achieved in 221 BCE, the First Emperor moved quickly to consolidate Qin rule. He deputed administrators throughout the realm to put in place a rational, centralized government; he instructed that local writing styles be unified and weights and measures be standardized; he had walls dividing the former independent states demolished and the roadways interconnected. Perhaps most famously of all, he ordered the construction of the Great Wall (see page 60), marking the northern boundary of the empire. And certainly most infamously, he ordered that all but technical literature should be proscribed; it is also said that he buried alive 400 scholars at court.

ABOVE **A bronze carriage and horses—one-third life-size—recovered in 1980 from a pit at Lintong, near Xi'an, Shaanxi, to the west of the tomb of the First Emperor, Qin Shi Huangdi. It was a separate find from the enormous terracotta army, which lay in a pit to the east and was unearthed five years previously (see photographs, pages 50–51).**

THE GREAT WALL OF CHINA

Having conquered all of the formerly independent states and thus unified China under a single government, the First Emperor of Qin ordered the construction of a great wall along the empire's northern frontier to protect against incursions from the Xiongnu, a powerful non-Chinese confederacy whose mastery of horsemanship had enabled them to dominate the steppe land of northeast and central Asia and contest power with the Chinese for several centuries. In fact, walls had already been built along much of this frontier by the independent states of the Warring States period; these were incorporated in the Qin Great Wall, at the same time that other of their walls, separating the states from each other, were demolished by the Qin as part of the emperor's process of national reunification.

The commander-in-chief of the Qin army, Meng Tian, deployed a force of some 300,000 soldiers and innumerable conscript laborers to build the wall. The wall, known as *wanli changcheng* (The Wall of Ten Thousand *Li*), was originally constructed of stamped earth, with watchtowers and barracks along its length, and extended from the Bay of Bohai in the east more than 3,700 miles (6,000 km), at its greatest historical extent, to the Jade Gate (Yumen) in the western desert province of Gansu.

Subsequent dynasties rebuilt walls along the northern frontier, sometimes on top of the old walls, sometimes in completely different locations. By no later than the Tang dynasty (618–907 CE), the Great Wall had already entered into the national consciousness as the dividing line between China and the outside world. The wall that survives today is not as long as it once was and has only been completely reconstructed or restored in several sections (shown here, right), including one in the hills at Badaling north of Beijing, and another at Mutianyu.

ACHIEVEMENTS OF HAN

ABOVE **A charming Han-dynasty painted pottery figurine of a kneeling entertainer. Figurines such as this, depicting a wide variety of lifetime experiences—from work to play—were put into tombs to accompany the dead into the afterlife.**

With the collapse of the Qin dynasty in 207 BCE, not long into the reign of its second emperor, China was thrown into a grueling five-year civil war between the forces of Xiang Yu (233–202 BCE), scion of a leading military family in the southern state of Chu, and Liu Bang (248–195 BCE), a local magistrate in eastern China. The forces of Liu Bang were ultimately victorious, and he established the Han dynasty, ruling as its High Ancestor (reigned 202–195 BCE).

The first generations of the Han dynasty were almost as turbulent as the years of the civil war. Internally, Liu Bang first divided power among his lieutenants, and then sought to take it back, replacing these confederates with fellow kinsmen of the Liu family. Externally, Liu Bang was even humiliated by the army of the Xiongnu leader (*shanyu*) Maodun (died 174 BCE), surviving with his life at the battle of Pingcheng only by way of a ruse. When Liu Bang died in 195 BCE from an arrow wound suffered in yet another battle, power passed to his consort, the Empress Lü (Lü Zhi, died 180 BCE). This succession caused yet another phase of civil unrest, with the Empress Lü first replacing, in a particularly violent manner, the Liu elite with members of her own Lü family, and then, after her death, with the Lius treating the Lü family in a similarly brutal fashion.

Still further civil disturbance wracked the country for the next several decades as the court sought to enhance its power vis-à-vis local rulers, even though those rulers were almost all from the same family. Finally, with the lengthy reign of Liu Che (reigned 141–87 BCE), more popularly known as Emperor Wu, central power was consolidated and, in addition, a series of military campaigns launched into Central Asia turned the balance of power against the Xiongnu and in favor of the Han.

Emperor Wu's reign was also notable for other reasons. Not only did he establish an imperial academy with the Confucian classics constituting the sole curriculum, but his era was blessed with a number of outstanding individuals, including—among the most illustrious—the philosopher and political theorist Dong Zhongshu (ca. 179–104 BCE), the poet Sima Xiangru (179–117 BCE), and the historian Sima Qian (145–ca. 86 BCE). In 104 BCE, the emperor performed rituals on Mount Tai, the sacred peak of the east, to mark the formal establishment of the dynasty.

Historians, beginning with Emperor Wu's contemporary Sima Qian, have not been uniformly positive in their assessment of the emperor. It has been suggested that toward the end of his lengthy reign he squandered much of the wealth and power that he had accumulated. During the century after his death, dynastic fortunes continued to decline, until in 9 CE Wang Mang (33 BCE–23 CE), the Marshall of State, usurped imperial privileges, establishing his own Xin dynasty (9–23 CE). Although the Han dynasty was restored in 25 CE, and persisted for almost another two hundred years (a time of many remarkable intellectual and technological developments, including the rise of Daoism, the introduction of Buddhism, and the invention of paper), imperial power diminished to the extent that the final emperor, Xian (reigned 189–220 CE), simply abdicated.

BELOW This green-glazed red pottery model is an example of a dwelling of the Han-dynasty period. Such models were particularly popular as grave goods for the later, or Eastern Han era.

CHINA'S EQUESTRIAN CULTURE

Although not indigenous to China, the horse has long played a vital role in the
country's military, social, and artistic history. Horse-drawn chariots were used by
the Shang from around 1200 BCE, but it was not until the Han and Tang dynasties
that man and horse became truly effective partners, in both recreation and war.
The transition of man to horseback rider meant that procuring or breeding horses
became a crucial feature of imperial policy. The illustrations above are based on
Han-dynasty sculptures, with the famous flying horse of Gansu shown center. The
mural, opposite, is a detail from the Tang-dynasty tomb of Prince Zhanghuai in Xi'an.

THREE KINGDOMS, SIX DYNASTIES

The demise of the four-hundred-year-long Han dynasty is often seen as a low point in the development of Chinese civilization. Even though the Han imperial insignia were turned over to the Marshall of State Cao Cao (155–220), who installed his son Cao Pi (187–226) as the first emperor of a newly established Wei dynasty (220–264), in fact China was at the time divided into three independent states: Wei, in charge of the former capitals and the northeast; Wu, dominant throughout the south; and Shu, located in the west in present-day Sichuan province. There ensued a sixty-year period of intermittent warfare, known in China as the period of the Three Kingdoms. When Wu was defeated in 280, the victor was neither Wei nor Shu, but another dynasty, the Jin (265–316 and 317–420). Like the Wei dynasty, the Jin was established by a family of warlords who forced the reigning emperor to abdicate. Also like the Wei, the Jin was short-lived: after just three reigns, its capitals were sacked in 311 and 316.

The Jin dynasty re-established itself as a power in the south of the country, ushering in the age known as the Six Dynasties (also known as the Northern and Southern dynasties). Nobles, the social elite, and commoners alike joined the Jin court there, setting in motion a demographic shift that was to transform China. Establishing a new capital at present-day Nanjing, south of the Yangzi river, the Eastern Jin dynasty (317–420) continued for another century, to be followed by several other even shorter-lived dynasties.

LEFT **A painted pottery figurine (Northern Wei dynasty) of a sturdy camel, saddled and ready for travel. As a result of the exotic goods they often carried on their backs, camels were strongly identified as symbols of wealth in China. From the Northern Wei dynasty on, they became increasingly popular as funerary objects.**

As unhappy as the short century of the Wei and Jin dynasties was as far as political history was concerned, it was one of the most vibrant periods in China in terms of philosophy, religion, and literature. Philosophers such as Wang Bi (226–249) made the period famous for *xuanxue*, "the study of the dark"—in other words, metaphysics; Daoism and Buddhism flourished; Ruan Ji (210–263), Ji Kang (223–262), and the other members of the group known as the "Seven Sages of the Bamboo Grove," helped to establish poetry as the foremost medium for the expression of personal sentiment. Presented with a lush, new intellectual landscape, poets turned more and more to nature, forgetting their political woes. The natural world obviously also inspired artists. No longer mere workmen in the employ of the court, painters such as Gu Kaizhi (345–411) developed landscapes (in Chinese, "mountains and rivers") as the preeminent style of Chinese painting.

Meanwhile, in the north of China, another series of short-lived and more local dynasties succeeded each other, many of them ruled by non-Chinese. The most important of these, the Toba or Tabgatch, in 386 established the capital of their Northern Wei (unrelated to the Wei) dynasty in Pingcheng (present-day Datong), in the far north of Shanxi province. They ruled there for a century, uniting all of north China and redistributing much of the population from the center to the periphery. In 494, they relocated their capital to Luoyang, site of the earlier capital of the Han, Wei, and Jin dynasties. It was the rulers of this Northern Wei dynasty who sponsored the Buddhist statues at Yungang (see pages 46–47), just outside of Datong, and at Longmen, near Luoyang (see photograph, page 45). In 534, the dynasty split, yielding in short order to two brief dynasties, Northern Qi and Northern Zhou.

ABOVE During the Northern Wei dynasty, the spread of Buddhism was pronounced and greatly encouraged. The gilt bronze figure (512 CE) shown here depicts a Buddhist *bodhisattva* ("enlightenment being") holding a sacred lotus in his right hand.

SUI AND TANG REVIVAL

The middle decades of the sixth century saw China not only divided between southern and northern dynasties, but also divided in the north among various generals. Finally, in 581, Yang Jian (541–604), one of the northern generals, succeeded in defeating his northern rivals and founded the Sui dynasty (581–618). Eight years later, he conquered southern China as well, reuniting China for the first time in almost three centuries.

The Sui is frequently compared with the Qin dynasty, the earlier unifier of the warring states. Like the Qin, the Sui is often criticized for the excessive costs of such massive public construction projects as the building of defensive walls and, especially, the Grand Canal, which succeeded in linking the Yangzi and Yellow rivers. Again like the Qin, the Sui was short-lived, its second emperor being overthrown (as also had been the second Qin emperor) in 618 by a peasant uprising. This uprising was led by Li Yuan (565–635), a general from northern Shanxi province, and his son, Li Shimin (598–649). Together they established the Tang dynasty (618–907), which would prove to be one of the greatest dynasties in Chinese history.

During the first decades of rule, the Tang made every effort to unite the country. Just as the Han dynasty had benefited from the construction projects undertaken during the preceding Qin dynasty, so too did the Tang benefit from the work done in the Sui. The two capitals of Chang'an and Luoyang, rebuilt on a grand scale by the Sui (the wall around Chang'an was 22 miles [35 km] in length), were supplied with the wealth of the south via the Grand Canal and with imported luxury items from central and western Asia via the Silk Road or Route. Chang'an, in particular, became a great cosmopolitan center, with a population of about a million people, including perhaps some 50,000 foreign merchants.

The first generations of the dynasty were not without their crises. Li Shimin forced his father to retire in 626. Then, some sixty years later, his one-time partner, Wu Zhao (better known by her reign name Wu Zetian), declared herself emperor of a new Zhou dynasty (690–705)—the only case in Chinese history of an officially declared female emperor. With the restoration of the Tang emperors, and especially with Emperor Xuanzong (reigned 712–756), the first half of the eighth century became perhaps the high tide of Chinese culture. It was the age of Li Bai (also known as Li Bo, 701–762) and Du Fu (712–770), China's two greatest poets ever; and the time of the monk Xuanzang's pilgrimage to India, which resulted in the translation into Chinese of more than 1,000 scrolls of Indian texts. However, Emperor Xuanzong's long reign ended finally in disaster, with a military revolt led by An Lushan (died 757), a general of mixed Sogdian-Turkic ancestry, and then a subsequent civil war that dragged on for eight years. Although the Tang emperors were restored yet again, and the dynasty persisted for another century and a half, in many respects the An Lushan Rebellion, as it is known, marks the end of China's ancient period.

RIGHT **A magnificent Tang-dynasty earthenware jar. The distinctive glaze used on the vessel is known as** *sancai* **("three colors") and is characteristic of the period. It consists of a clear glaze; an amber glaze, made from iron oxide; and a bright green glaze, made from copper oxide. The glazes have been encouraged to run around the contours of the vessel, producing this wonderfully vibrant, graphic design.**

THE CAVES OF THE THOUSAND *BUDDHAS*

Dunhuang and its Caves of the Thousand *Buddha*s (Qian Fo Dong) is one of the most famous sites in China, despite its remote location beyond the western terminus of the Great Wall in far western Gansu. The site actually owes both its existence and its fame to this location. Dunhuang was first made a Chinese administrative district after Emperor Wu of the Han dynasty (reigned 141–87 BCE) succeeded in extending Chinese control into Central Asia (see pages 62–63). With the subsequent development of trade along the Silk Road, its location at the eastern confluence of the northern and southern routes (those that followed the Tian Shan and Kunlun Shan mountain ranges respectively) made it a wealthy trading center.

From the 4th century CE, monks from throughout China and Central Asia gathered in this area, carving Buddhist temple-caves into a ridge of the Mingsha Shan (Singing Sands Mountain), some 20 miles (32 km) outside the town of Dunhuang. The caves feature clay statuary of *buddha*s and *bodhisattva*s ("enlightenment beings") and murals on the surrounding walls. The paintings, in particular, display much of the early development of Chinese painting styles, with good examples of high Tang realism in portraiture and the beginnings of perspective in landscape painting. The photograph shown here (right), from Cave 285, dates from the early 6th century CE and depicts the Buddha (central niche) flanked by two monks. A spectacular array of Hindu divinities—including Shiva, Ganesha, Vishnu, and Indra—surround the niches. The room is thought to have been a meditation chamber.

In addition to the exceptional works of art contained within the caves, Dunhuang is also famous for the thousands of manuscripts, in various languages, and dating from the 5th to 10th centuries (see page 22). Because of the arid desert climate, the manuscripts, like the paintings in the caves, have been preserved in almost perfect condition.

LIFE IN ANCIENT CHINA

LEFT A late-Tang-dynasty wall painting from Cave 9 at Dunhuang, Gansu, which gives a "bird's-eye view" of a courtyard residence, in this case one used for business purposes. In addition to being a Buddhist center, Dunhuang was an important commercial hub where the two branches of the Silk Road converged, and the salesmen who traveled along it brought considerable wealth. The scene offers an informative depiction of an elite Chinese house with its exterior wall and rooms opening on interior courtyards, where—even in Central Asia—bamboo grows.

In ancient China, lives were lived within the context of the family. One was not just a child, but rather a son or daughter; not just an adult, but rather a father or mother; and, if fortunate, not just a senior citizen, but rather a grandfather or grandmother. It was from the family that one learned society's core values: that hierarchies are natural but not static; that social harmony should be placed above personal desires; and that eternal life requires corporate effort. Nevertheless, there were also significant rites of passage to mark individual lives, from birth and acceptance into the family, through attainment of adulthood and marriage, to old age and, finally, death and burial. This last passage, death, was regarded, at least by the majority of people, as perhaps the most important one— to the realm of the ancestors and spirits.

BELOW A Tang-dynasty pottery figurine. Such artifacts provide invaluable information on the type of makeup, hairstyles, and dress that was popular at the time.

BIRTH AND CHILDHOOD

As is perhaps fitting, records of birth-giving go back to the very beginning of the Chinese historical tradition. The oracle-bone inscriptions from the Shang dynasty king Wu Ding (ca. 1200 BCE) include divinations concerning at least three pregnancies of his consort Fu Hao. In one case, which the king prognosticated to be inauspicious, a post-natal verification confirmed that "it really was inauspicious; it was a girl." In later times, it appears that the role of women was somewhat more highly valued—if only for the fact that they gave birth to the all-important sons. The mother of Mencius (ca. 390–305 BCE)—who was, after Confucius himself, the most influential Confucian philosopher in antiquity—is renowned for instructing her son, while still in her womb, on the values of leading an ethical life.

Soon after an infant's entry into the world, he or she became subject to the rituals often associated with Confucianism. The *Record of Rituals* states that on the child's third day of life, divinations were to be performed to determine which male should "raise up" the child and carry it outside the birthing chamber. Perhaps inevitably in a traditional society a number of children— males born with birth defects that would render them incapable of performing ancestral rituals, some girls, and some babies born to parents too poor to care for them—were not raised up, but abandoned. Cruel though this may seem, and there is some evidence to suggest that in the Qin dynasty (221–207 BCE) this practice was regarded as a crime, it is grounded in fundamental Chinese notions of human nature, which hold that one's nature (that is, one's life) is a process: one is not born a fully evolved human being, and infancy marks only the initial coalescence of the life forces.

For those youths who were accepted into the family, education seems to have

LEFT A terracotta statue of an apparently pregnant woman, 4th–6th century CE. Although there was usually great delight at the prospect of childbirth in ancient China, the actual process itself was thought to be unclean. The birth would therefore usually take place away from the home to avoid the risk of contamination. In households of the elite, post-natal care would sometimes be placed in the hands of servants and wet nurses.

been an overriding concern—at least with respect to the elite families who make up the bulk of the dynastic histories. For example, Ban Gu (32–92 CE), who would go on to write the *Book of Han*, is said to have memorized the *Classic of Poetry* by the age of eight, and also to have been proficient in writing his own poetry. Young girls were educated in "female morals" and song and dance, but it was not unheard of that they too should become literate and, in some—admittedly rare—cases achieve literary renown; thus, Ban Zhao (48–ca. 116 CE) completed the *Book of Han* that had been started by her brother Ban Gu.

BELOW This delightful wooden Han-dynasty ox and cart would doubtless have appealed to adults and children alike. Among the many ancient Chinese toys to have been discovered are masks, marbles, puppets, and numerous animals, such as lions and dragons.

LINEAGES OF MALES

BELOW Two Tang-dynasty three-color pottery figurines of soldiers in full armor. Throughout much of ancient China, armies were manned primarily by conscripts who were obliged to perform government service for a certain period of time each year. During the Tang dynasty this began to change as large standing garrisons of professional soldiers were established to guard the frontiers.

Men were pre-eminent in all spheres of public life in ancient China: government officials from the emperor to the lowliest clerk were all males, as were intellectuals, such as philosophers and historians, poets and painters, and those whom we know to have contributed to the development of Buddhism and Daoism. Most artisans and merchants were also males. In the private sphere, too, males were regarded as uniquely responsible for the perpetuation of the family line—the most important social value of all. This responsibility centered on the sacrifices performed in the all-male ancestral temple.

The establishment of China's ancestral system is traditionally credited to the Duke of Zhou (ca. 1085–1032 BCE), a younger brother of King Wu of Zhou (reigned 1049–1043 BCE) and one of the founding fathers of the Zhou dynasty. Although ancestors certainly figured importantly in the divinations of the preceding Shang dynasty, it would seem that this tradition is accurate, at least in its timing; the early Zhou bronze inscriptions attest to the central role the ancestral temple played in the country's political and social life, and poems in the *Classic of Poetry* provide glimpses of the activities that took place there.

Ancient China's kinship system was simultaneously simple and complicated. During the Zhou dynasty, there were only about twenty different family surnames, but within each family there were numerous lineages and branch lineages, each of which

replicated the kinship structure of the family; in time, these lineages would in fact become independent families. The ancestral temple was dedicated in the first place to the historical person considered to be the founder of the family or the lineage. Thus, for the royal Zhou Ji family, the ancestral temple in the capital was dedicated to King Wen (reigned 1099–1051 BCE). Subsequent generations of ancestors were arrayed in the temple, in alternating generations, either side of the high ancestor. The name given to this left–right alternation is *zhao–mu*, probably taken from the reign-names of the two Zhou kings when the system was put firmly in place—King Zhao (reigned 977–957 BCE) and King Mu (reigned 956–918 BCE). It specified that one's place in the temple was not beside one's father, but beside one's grandfather. For this reason, it was the eldest grandson who was featured in the ancestor sacrifices, since he was considered to be the personification of his grandfather (for the purposes of the sacrifice, he was referred to as the "corpse"). After a certain number of generations (seven for the royal family, five for the nobility, and three for the lesser aristocracy), ancestors other than the high ancestor would be displaced from the central temple and grouped together in one of two side chambers. Also after a number of generations (five seems to have been the norm), younger brothers—who were excluded from the rituals of the ancestral temple—might establish branch lineages, and become high ancestors in their own right.

ABOVE **Affairs of state were very much a male enterprise in ancient China, as suggested in this detail of a grouping of mandarins (left) and foreign envoys, from a Tang-dynasty mural decorating the east wall of the tomb of Prince Zhanghuai in Xi'an. The image is also indicative of the attempts that were made to foster friendly diplomatic relations between China and the outside world—the envoy at right is identifiable as being from the northern Korean kingdom of Koguryo—during the Tang dynasty.**

THE ROLES OF WOMEN

In the Chinese conception of the world, all energy and matter was made up of two natures, *yin* and *yang*. These originally referred to shade and sunshine, but by an early period had been extended to an almost infinite series of oppositions: cold and hot, wet and dry, inner and outer, private and public, and, of course, female and male. Many have contended that this gave rise to an essentially misogynistic conception that was responsible for keeping women hidden and very much out of public view. An alternative view regards *yin* and *yang* as complementary, with both being necessary to complete the circle of life. Both these views are overly simplified.

LEFT Detail from an anonymous painting of the 10th century CE, entitled *Banquet and Concert*, **depicting magnificently attired women of the Tang imperial court enjoying music and a fine feast. When not in attendance at entertainments, women at court were generally sequestered in their living quarters, situated at the rear of the palace, where they had charge of the imperial offspring.**

It is certainly true that on the rare occasions that Chinese women entered into public life—especially political life—it is almost always portrayed as an aberration, usually with very unhappy consequences. The falls of the Shang and Western Zhou dynasties are routinely blamed on the final emperors' infatuation with women; and both the great Han and Tang dynasties were almost cut short when imperial consorts actually usurped power. But there is reason to believe that women's roles were also appreciated. The tombs of some women were certainly lavishly furnished with grave goods, as was the case with the Shang-dynasty tomb of Fu Hao (died ca. 1195 BCE) and the two Han-dynasty tombs of the ladies Dai (died ca. 165 BCE, see page 97) and Dou (died ca. 115 BCE), found at Mawangdui and Mancheng. We know too from the oracle-bone inscriptions that Fu Hao was a very active participant in the life at court—not only were there divinations about her giving birth, as we might expect, but there were also divinations that related to her raising troops and even leading them into battle. It is true that this is an exceptional case, and one, moreover, that was unknown throughout traditional times.

However, the lives of other women were remembered. Although written by a man (Liu Xiang [ca. 76–8 BCE]), one much-read work, *Biographies of Estimable Women*, narrates the lives of 125 notable women who lived from early antiquity down to the time of the book's compilation in 16 BCE. For example, the mother of Mencius, the philosopher, was praised for overseeing her son's education. The first work we know of to have been written wholly by a woman, the *Admonitions for Women* by Ban Zhao (48–ca. 116 CE), was conservative in tone, consisting of instructions to women as to their correct conduct in marriage, thereby ensuring they kept to their rightful place. This set the tone for a genre of "women's books," written by both men and women.

THE ART OF ADORNMENT

The elite of ancient China were keen to surround themselves with magnificent objects, and especially to wear them. The subtle beauty of materials such as jade and silk was preferred to ostentatious displays of gold and silver. Jade was fashioned into many types of jewelry, such as this glorious Tang-dynasty pendant (above). Glass beads (right) were strung into necklaces, and hair clasps (as left, in bronze, inlaid with gold and turquoise) were produced from various media. Silk came in every imaginable color and design. Clothing was intended to be more than just appealing—it was regarded as the outward sign of the wearer's inner virtue and was symbolic of his or her status in life, as indicated by the elegant attire of the women (one of whom is using a hair pin) represented on this Tang-dynasty mural (opposite).

MARRIAGE

In ancient China, marriage was usually a more corporate endeavor than just the union of one man and one woman. For ordinary people, evidence suggests that there were communal gatherings of young men and young women, sometimes in the spring and sometimes in the autumn, which, after an exchange of songs and love tokens, ended in dances, and often much more. For the elite, however, marriage was very much viewed as the union of two families. Indeed, during the Zhou period (1045–256 BCE), the bride was usually accompanied by her sisters or female cousins, who would serve as secondary wives. In all periods, a man was free to have as many women (as distinct from secondary wives) as his family could afford (though the primary wife enjoyed all of the privileges of the marriage).

Marriage relations required the services of an intermediary, or *mei*. Brides-to-be, presented with slippers made of *kudzu* (a vine with various uses related to pregnancy and birth), would perform a dance, re-enacting the way in which Jiang Yuan, the progenitress of the Zhou people, was thought to have become pregnant by stepping in God's footprint. Following the dance, arrows would be placed into quivers hanging from the women's girdle sash (the symbolism of which was obvious).

The ritual texts describe a more sedate ceremony. The groom, who was supposed to have waited until the age of thirty before marrying, would call on the bride's family. He did so in the evening, in part because the word for evening, *hun*, was homophonous with the word for marriage, and in part because evening was the onset of darkness—according to the ancient Chinese notion of *yin–yang* duality, darkness and women were both *yin*, and so night was the proper time for the bride to come. The groom bore a present of a wild goose (or, better, a pair of them), because geese were supposed to mate for life. He would first confirm that the bride's surname was not the same as his own. In ancient times, there were even fewer surnames in China than there are now, which was a limiting factor. After taking the bride back to his own family, the marriage would be consummated, first with a banquet. After three months, the marriage would be regarded as completed and the wife assumed her privileges and responsibilities in her husband's family.

LEFT Mid-Tang-dynasty mural from Cave 25 at Yulin ku, Gansu, depicting a bride (kneeling at right) and groom (standing beside her) presenting themselves to the groom's parents. In the foreground are three bride's attendants, and in the background a servant of the parents. The ceremony takes places inside a yurt or tent-like room, and all of the participants are dressed in Tibetan clothing. At the time of this painting (8th century), Tibet was a great power, controlling not only all of present-day Tibet but also much of Central Asia, including the present-day Chinese province of Gansu.

THE WORLD OF WORK

There were four main categories of workers in ancient Chinese society: farmers, soldiers, artisans, and merchants; they were usually ranked in this order, although soldiers sometimes received the top billing. It is perhaps ironic that virtually all the country's magnificent cultural artifacts were produced by artisans and were paid for, either directly or indirectly, by merchants—in other words, the two least respected classes of workers.

Ranked over these four classes was, of course, the ruling nobility. Such rulers were necessary because work, like most aspects of life in ancient China, was almost always a corporate undertaking, and as such required constant administration. According to mythology, Yu the Great dredged the watercourses by himself (see pages 31–32), but in reality, armies of workers were mobilized by each succeeding state to keep the Yellow river within ever-higher levees. Other projects demanded even greater manpower. The story of the Qin general Meng Tian taking an army of 300,000 soldiers and conscript laborers to the northern frontier to construct the Great Wall is, of course, infamous, but by no means isolated. Even in neolithic times, most cities were furnished with high city walls, all of them constructed by peasants pressed into service when not in their fields. It has been estimated that the wall that was built around the fourteenth-century BCE Shang city at

LEFT **A Sui-dynasty ceramic model showing potters at work. The eponymous text written by Mencius provided a rationale for both the division of labor and a hierarchical society. Challenged by one Xu Xing, a contemporary anarchist, to eat only food that he had grown himself, Mencius asked Xu if he should use only earthenware pots that he made himself to cook his food. Xu allowed that he could go to a potter. Just as there is a need for potters to do this work, so too, argued Mencius, is there a need for administrators to govern society.**

Zhengzhou, Henan—a Shang capital prior to their move to Anyang—required 10,000 laborers to work every day for twelve and a half years. Artisans, too, must often have worked in groups that required considerable coordination. The casting of a bronze vessel, for example, would have required not only potters to shape the model and mold, and smelters to smelt the copper, tin, and lead ore, but also—in the case of a large vessel, which could reach a weight of several hundred pounds—a great many menial laborers just to pour the molten bronze into the assembly.

But it was in the arena of war that the need for administration was the greatest, and had the greatest repercussions for the state as a whole. There is a romantic notion that in the glory days of the early Zhou dynasty, warfare was an elite affair, undertaken by a handful of charioteers. Although this is almost certainly an underestimation, it is true that by the Warring States period (480–222 BCE) warfare had developed into a quite different affair: confrontations were now between massed infantry armies, often involving hundreds of thousands of soldiers. The logistics of putting such armies into the field gave rise to both professional generals and to books of administrative science. It was perhaps the mastery of this science, more than any other single factor, that allowed the state of Qin to conquer all the other warring states, and then to lay the foundation for the Chinese imperial bureaucracy.

ABOVE The remains of earthen and adobe walls at the ancient city of Gaochang—near Turfan, Xinjiang region—that once served as a major commercial and cultural center on the northern edge of the Silk Road (see pages 122–123). The city was divided into three areas: an outer city with nine gates, an inner city, and the palace grounds. The street pattern within the massive surrounding walls was well ordered. The actual construction of such cities would have necessitated the deployment of a massive labor force.

IN PURSUIT OF LEISURE

Just as Wellington's victory over Napoleon was said to have been won on the playing fields of Eton school, so too was much Chinese play a preparation for the serious game of war. The first games for which we have evidence were archery contests. The Zha Bo *gui*, a Zhou bronze vessel (produced around 1000 BCE and discovered in 1993 at Pingdingshan, Henan), was cast to commemorate Zha Bo's victory in one such contest. The inscription states that the king held up a prize and announced that it would go to the winner; Zha Bo then shot ten times, hitting the target each time. Throughout the remainder of early antiquity, archery remained one of the six arts that all educated men were expected to master (the other arts were those of the lute, the chariot, the writing brush, mathematics, and the rites). Some, at least, recognized that it was just a game. Criticized for being an empty-headed philosopher, Confucius (551–479 BCE) asked in jest exactly what his critic would have him master—chariotry or archery. He then answered his own question by announcing that, fine, he would go off and practice his driving.

ABOVE **A detail from a 25-foot (8-m) long mural of an imperial hunting party, from the Tang-dynasty tomb of Prince Zhanghuai in Xi'an. Hunting on horseback was a popular leisure activity among the elite; it often involved several hundred riders at a time and provided ideal military training.**

Other games required still greater athletic prowess. During the Han dynasty, a form of wrestling called *juedi* was enjoyed both at court and in the markets. Since the name means "horns linked" and suggests a face-off between two bulls or two rams, it seems to have been something like the sumo wrestling found in Japan. During the Tang dynasty, polo enjoyed even greater popularity among the elites, and was depicted in murals that adorned the walls of tombs. Another elite pastime also shown in the murals is the grand hunt, involving hundreds of persons on horseback and strikingly reminiscent of the English fox hunt (see illustration, above).

RIGHT An impish court jester is portrayed in this Eastern Han-dynasty terracotta model. The emperor and his courtiers would often be entertained by such figures who, it is claimed, sometimes attempted to subtly influence the opinions of their rulers by means of their comic performances. Other forms of court entertainment included song-and-dance productions, acrobatics, various tests of strengths, and—especially in the Tang-dynasty period— exhibitions of exotic animals.

There were more cerebral games as well. One of these represented for us by Han tomb figurines was called *liubo* (see page 88); it seems to have combined elements of skill and chance, the board on which it was played resembling also a diviner's board used in determining astrological omens. Another board game (again, a simulation of warfare) was *weiqi*, variants of which are known in the West as "Chinese chess." *Weiqi* seems to have been played throughout China's antiquity, but it reached something of a fever pitch at the time of Emperor Wu of the Liang dynasty (reigned 502–550 CE). Emperor Wu himself was a great aficionado of the game, often playing all night with his ministers, and writing various treatises on the game, at least one of which seems to have been preserved. Emperor Wu also once organized a national tournament of *weiqi*. It is a testament to his sense of fair play that even though he participated in the tournament, he did not emerge as the victor.

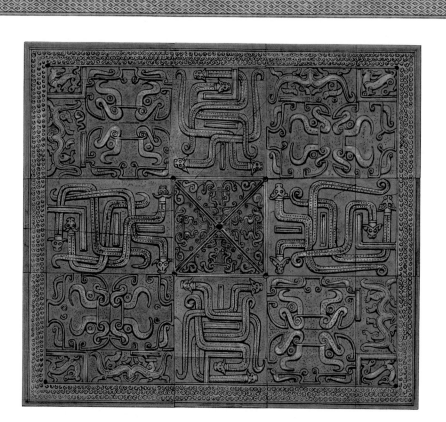

LIUBO: COSMIC DICE GAME

Both literary references and artifactual evidence suggest that the game of *liubo* (thought to mean "six dice") was one of the most popular entertainments during the late Warring States period and throughout the Han dynasty. It was played on a board conceived as a representation of the universe. The stone board shown above is an example from the Warring States period. Two players threw the eighteen-sided dice (see right and left) in turn, and then moved their twelve game pieces, six dragons and six tigers—the Eastern Han-dynasty pottery model, opposite, depicts two figures engrossed in the game. Unfortunately, by the sixth century CE, the rules seem to have been lost; even Yan Zhitui (531–ca. 591), who had an almost encyclopedic knowledge of ancient traditions, admitted that he did not know how to play.

OLD AGE

A Han-dynasty incense burner of the type known as a "Universal Mountain Censer" (*Boshan lu*). In ancient China, mountains were considered to be meeting places of Earth and the heavens, and climbing them was one way for people to ascend to heaven. Here the mountain is perched on the head of a bird, which stands in turn on the back of a turtle, whose symbolism includes longevity and strength. In Chinese mythology, one of the original pillars of heaven was broken when Gong Gong, rebelling against the Yellow Emperor, butted into Mount Incomplete (Buzhou shan). Nü Wa, sister/wife of Fuxi, restored the pillar by stacking turtleshells. Because of this, turtles are often depicted holding up such things as stone steles.

Bronze inscriptions of the Western Zhou period routinely conclude with a prayer addressed to the deceased grandfather and father of the vessel's patron to bestow on him "august longevity." Later inscriptions, from about the time of Confucius, invoke the longevity of the Duke of Shao, one of the founding fathers of the Zhou dynasty, and there is in fact evidence that he lived a very long life, perhaps more than one hundred years. In an age when the average life expectancy was probably about forty-five years, this must have seemed very old indeed. And although grandfathers were always invoked in prayer, it was probably quite rare that one lived to see one's own grandchildren.

Those who did live to old age in ancient China enjoyed not just the respect of their descendants, but also a number of socially sanctioned privileges. The Confucian text *Mencius* states as a matter of objective fact that all elders are owed respect simply because of their age. The same text also indicates that those who reached the age of fifty were to be clothed in silk, and those who reached seventy were to receive meat with their meals; this latter privilege would have been enjoyed by other members of the family only at the feasts following offerings to the ancestors. Outside of the family, the law code of the Qin dynasty, discovered in 1975 in the tomb of a Qin local magistrate, specified that men over the age of sixty were exempt from all forms of unpaid labor, and were also to receive pardons from certain forms of punishment.

Around the time that Mencius (ca. 390–305 BCE) was writing about elders, other philosophers were suggesting that special diets, gymnastics, and breathing techniques could contribute to one's longevity. By the Han period, "masters of recipes" competed to invent new means to prolong life, especially for their imperial patrons. This led to the development of the alchemical attempt to convert base metals into gold, in the hope that ingesting the concoction would endow the body with the incorruptible properties attributed to the precious metal.

In later antiquity, experiments such as these were usually associated with Daoism. Although their many failures often caused others to heap scorn on Daoists, such efforts nevertheless led to notable developments in both religion and science. By the beginning of the Tang dynasty, Daoists were practicing "internal alchemy," an attempt to transform the substances of their own bodies by means of meditation, breath control, and yoga, and this in turn contributed greatly to meditational practices. About the same time, "external alchemists," who were involved in experimentation with chemicals, were responsible for significant advancements in science and technology in China. The mixing of sulphur and saltpeter, for example, was first documented in the fourth century CE. When carbon was added to this mixture in the ninth century, gunpowder was created—this was but one of several notable inventions inspired by the external alchemists.

ABOVE **A gold seal in the shape of a turtle, from the Western Han-dynasty tomb of the king of Nanyue, excavated in Guangzhou (Canton), Guangdong. Both the turtle and gold were symbols of longevity and purity, the turtle for being the longest lived of animals (it was often noted in early texts that the word for "turtle" was anciently homophonous with the word for "old"), and gold for its incorruptibility. Gold was never very plentiful in ancient China, and this perhaps gave rise by the Six Dynasties period to the science of alchemy, the attempt to transform base substances into gold.**

DEATH AND THE TWO SOULS

The popular conception of the human body in ancient China—as opposed to the elite medical conception—was that it is made up of two different types of elements or souls. One, called the *po*, was viscous and material; the other, called the *hun*, was vaporous and ethereal. It was thought that the convergence of these two types of souls produced life, and that their dispersion brought death. The *hun* souls, being lighter and more prone to depart from the body (which they did in deep sleep, their wanderings being the cause of dreams), were the first to leave at the time of death. Immediately after the apparent death of a person, the son would climb to the roof of the house to "summon" the *hun* souls to return. Only when this ritual failed to revive the person was he or she definitively declared to be "dead."

The deceased was then prepared for the tomb and efforts were made to preserve the body. At the very least, jade, the finest of all stones, was inserted into the mouth to stop the decaying process. In other cases, the corpse was dressed with an entire shroud of jade pieces. In one notable archaeological discovery of 1971, Lady Dai (died ca. 165 BCE), the wife of the king of Changsha in the early years of the Han dynasty, was found almost perfectly preserved in her tomb at Mawangdui, apparently the result of a deliberate mummification process. But for most people, it was understood that death entailed the decomposition of the body. This is why tombs were dug into the soil, close to the subterranean Yellow Springs, the abode of the dead. The material substance of the body would be transported there when the viscous *po* souls departed the body and flowed downward through the ground.

One amusing story in the *Zuo zhuan* or *Zuo's Tradition*, a narrative history of the Spring and Autumn period, reveals the nature of the popular belief. Lady Jiang of Shen married Duke Wu of Zheng and gave birth to two sons, the future Duke

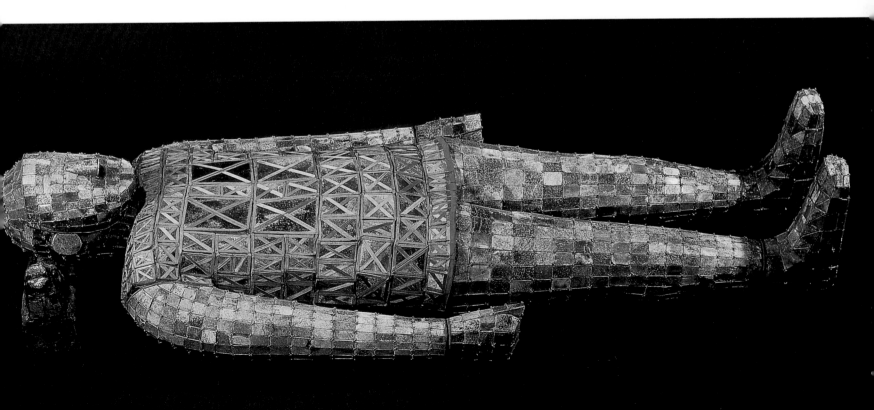

Zhuang and his younger brother Duan. Lady Jiang always favored Duan, and once even colluded with him in a plot to overthrow Duke Zhuang. Learning of the plot, the duke sent his brother into exile and confined his mother, swearing an oath that he would not again look upon her face until they met in the Yellow Springs. However, after entertaining a commoner who set aside a portion of his dinner so he could share it with his mother, Duke Zhuang came to bitterly regret his decision. But as a ruler, he could not breach his oath. The commoner therefore devised a plan whereby the duke could both keep his word and also meet with his mother. He had pits dug down to the water table by the Yellow Springs, with a perpendicular tunnel connecting them. Duke Zhuang and his mother each went to the bottom of one of the pits (that is, to the Yellow Springs) and there made peace with each other.

BELOW **The body of Princess Dou Wan (wife of Liu Sheng, king of the state of Zhongshan) was enclosed within this magnificent jade burial suit, following her death in around 100 BCE. Jade was thought to prevent decomposition and was therefore often used in various ways in burial procedures, including being placed in the mouth of the deceased.**

EQUIPPED FOR THE HEREAFTER

The archaeology of China is overwhelmingly mortuary in nature, probably more so than in any other culture. In a land where almost all buildings were made of wood and most of which has been continuously occupied since neolithic times, few structures above ground have survived the ravages of time and man. Fortunately, despite admonitions in various early texts against great expenditures on burials, many of the tens of thousands of tombs Chinese archaeologists have unearthed in the past century have been very lavishly furnished. We owe most of our advances in the understanding of ancient China to the structure and contents of these tombs.

RIGHT A view of the brick-vaulted, multichambered interior of the Western Han-period tomb at Holingor, Inner Mongolia. The northerly region was the location for garrisons and this tomb was built to house the mortal remains of a high-ranking army officer. Although poorly preserved, the surviving wall murals depict scenes from the deceased's career and everyday life.

Burial practice underwent considerable change over the course of China's antiquity. During the Shang and Western Zhou periods, tombs were essentially vertical shafts dug into the ground. They were differentiated, of course, according to size and furnishings. All of the tombs of Shang kings at Anyang were plundered in antiquity, probably soon after the Zhou conquest, and the tombs of the Zhou kings have never been found (though latest reports suggest that this may soon change). However, the tomb of Fu Hao (died ca. 1195 BCE, see page 5), one of the consorts of the Shang king Wu Ding (ca. 1200 BCE), gives some idea of what they may have contained. Although her tomb was modest in size by Shang royal standards, when excavated in 1975 it revealed over 440 bronzes, 590 jade carvings, nearly 7,000 cowrie shells, and evidence of sixteen humans who had been sacrificed to her.

By the early Warring States period, the first signs appear of what would become a complete change in tomb architecture. The tomb of Lord Yi of Zeng (died 433 BCE) was still essentially a vertical shaft, even if a very large one; but for the first time, in addition to the coffin chamber, the tomb also included two side chambers furnished with equipment to ensure that he could continue to enjoy in the afterlife many of the pleasures to which he had become accustomed on Earth.

By the Han dynasty, tombs of elites became veritable microcosms of the universe. Many now included multiple chambers, constructed with brick or stone walls. Some boasted vaulted ceilings, on which were painted the sun and the moon, the stars and planets. The walls were carved with hortatory scenes from history, suggesting the deceased's virtue by association. By the Tang dynasty, these stone carvings gave way to life-sized painted murals depicting the opulence of Tang life and revealing the skill of ancient Chinese painters.

THE INFLUENTIAL AFTERLIFE

Both the oracle-bone inscriptions of the Shang dynasty and the bronze inscriptions of the Zhou dynasty attest to the influence that the dead continued to have over the world of the living. Divinations suggest that reigning Shang kings believed that their recently deceased ancestors regularly caused them trouble, from floods of the Huan river, which flowed through Anyang, to royal toothaches. On the other hand, more distant ancestors were perceived to be beneficent, capable of interceding with Di, the Shang high god, to provide divine aid with the harvest, city building, and military campaigns, among other state enterprises. The Zhou people seem generally to have regarded all their ancestors as benign spirits, residing in heaven. The Confucian (hence, Chinese) obligation of filial piety that all sons owed their living fathers and mothers developed out of an earlier tradition of making offerings to ancestors (a tradition that never ceased).

Other evidence offers a different perspective on the relationship between the living and dead. A tomb at Fangmatan, in China's western province of Gansu, contained various kinds of texts, including probably the earliest existing ghost story in China. The text describes how a man named Dan was allowed to return to life after it was determined that his death by suicide had been premature. Dan reported on some of the likes and dislikes of the dead: "The dead do not want many clothes. People think that wrapping offerings in white cogon-grass makes them auspicious, but ghosts think offerings are auspicious no matter how they are wrapped. But those who offer sacrifices ought not to spit. If they spit, the ghosts flee in fright."

With the coming of Buddhism in the first centuries of the common era, and especially with the importation of its intricate notions of reincarnation and retribution, indigenous Chinese notions of "hungry ghosts" took on new meaning. Now

This Han-dynasty silk funerary banner was found placed over the coffin of Lady Dai (died ca. 165 BCE), the wife of the king of Changsha, in her tomb at Mawangdui, Hunan province. The banner's three main sections represent heaven, Earth, and the netherworld. In the middle (earthly) section, Lady Dai is shown (attended by servants) progressing upward on her journey from life—in itself a clear indication of a pre-Buddhist Chinese belief in the soul's ascension to heaven after death.

both Buddhism and Daoism described purgatorial afterlives, complete with judges and jailers, who would punish the dead for sins committed during their lives. One of the most popular tales of the Tang dynasty tells of the quest by Mulian (in Sanskrit, Maudgalyayana), the disciple of the Buddha most adept at supernatural powers, to find his deceased mother. Descending through the gates of the Yellow Springs (see page 92), Mulian passes through layer after layer of purgatories, all described in terrifying detail. He finally finds her in the deepest of all hells, the Avici Hell, where her body is nailed down with forty-nine long, metal spikes. The mother, remanded there for sins committed in past lives, is always ravenously hungry, since food cannot pass through her now needle-thin neck. Whenever Mulian offers her food at the ancestral temple, it always bursts into flames upon reaching her mouth. Eventually, Mulian petitions the Buddha, who teaches him to make offerings to hungry monks on the fifteenth day of the seventh month. When Mulian does this, thus inaugurating one of the most important Buddhist feast days in China, his mother is released to live in the highest heaven.

THE TOMB OF EMPRESS WU

Wu Zhao, better known as Wu Zetian (died 705 CE), is one of the most fascinating, even if reviled, figures in Chinese history. She was a consort to both emperors Taizong and Gaozong of the Tang dynasty, becoming Gaozong's empress. When he suffered a stroke in 660, she quickly consolidated power into her own hands. After his death in 683, she first put her own son on the throne, but within a few years declared herself emperor of a newly established Zhou dynasty, becoming the only woman in Chinese history to have ruled in her own right. A devout Buddhist, Wu Zetian took advantage of the political, economic, and ideological support of the Buddhist church to secure her power (she was widely viewed as a reincarnation of the *bodhisattva* Maitreya, the Buddhist saviour). She made Buddhism the state religion, founded monasteries, and subsidized translation projects and the making of huge quantities of religious art.

The imposing figures shown here (opposite) are the stone attendants that stand guard outside Wu Zetian's burial mound at Qianling, Shaanxi. The tomb, which she shares with Emperor Gaozong, has a pyramidal tumulus, symbolic of her imperial status. This style of tomb, most often identified with the tomb of Qin Shi Huang, the First Emperor, but seen also with the tombs of both the Han and Tang emperors, may well have been inspired by the pyramids of Egypt. The earliest example in China, the mausoleum of the rulers of Zhongshan at Pingshan, Hebei province, dates to the end of the fourth century BCE, just a generation later than the celebrated tomb of King Mausolus (reigned 377–353 BCE) at Halicarnassus, Bodrum, modern-day Turkey.

ARTS AND LETTERS

LEFT A human face
decorates each side of a late
Shang-dynasty rectangular
bronze *ding*, or cauldron
(see page 16), 1200–1000 BCE,
unearthed from Ningxian,
Hunan province. There is
at least some suggestion
that another rectangular
ding discovered in Anyang
and also decorated with
the human face might
have been used to make
human offerings.

The ancient Chinese created masterpieces of artistic expression in most of the many media known to humankind. Their exquisitely crafted work in lacquer, silk, and jade constitutes a unique contribution to world culture. But their tremendous artistic and intellectual legacy extends still further: from the pottery of the Yangshao neolithic culture to Tang-dynasty tomb murals; from intricately ornamented bronze vessels to colossal stone sculptures of the Buddha; and from a philosophy that united heaven, Earth, and humans to a highly distinctive style of cooking. These various traditions developed, sometimes along similar lines, sometimes in different directions, in a grand pro-fusion. Together they present an enticing vision of a rich and fascinating culture.

BELOW A leaping glass fish
from the Han dynasty.
Associated with good
fortune, longevity, literary
skills, and scholarship, the
fish was a popular motif in
ancient Chinese art. Its
decorative, graceful form
can be found adorning
numerous artifacts in
pottery, bronze, jade,
lacquerwork, and silk.

THE FINEST OF STONES: JADE

The *Discussion of Pictographs and Analysis of Characters* (*Shuo wen jie zi*), China's first dictionary, written by Xu Shen and presented at court in 100 CE, includes the following entry for jade: "The finest of stones, it embraces the five virtues: clarity is typified by its luster, bright yet warm; rectitude by its translucence, revealing the color and patterns within; wisdom by the purity and penetrating quality of its sound when struck; courage in that it can be broken but not bent; and equity in that it has sharp edges that do not injure." As the Chinese language evolved, the word "jade" was applied to the finest and most mysterious of things, among which were objects used by the emperor, the moon, women, and also, of course, the highest deity in the Daoist religion, the Jade Emperor.

The stone had a long history of use in China. Museum collections around the

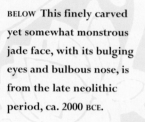

BELOW **This finely carved yet somewhat monstrous jade face, with its bulging eyes and bulbous nose, is from the late neolithic period, ca. 2000 BCE.**

world include thousands of pieces that everyone agreed were old, even very old, but no one knew just how ancient. Archaeological discoveries in the last forty years or so have provided some of the cultural context for these artifacts. Numerous sites of the Liangzhu culture have been excavated in Zhejiang province. The oldest of the sites date to the late fifth millennium BCE, and contain jades of exquisite workmanship in forms that would undergo little change for the next 4,000 years. Among them are circular disks, or *bi*, and rectangular blocks, *cong* (see caption, right), that are believed to have ritual significance. Very different jades have been found at the other end of China, in the far northern provinces of Liaoning and Inner Mongolia. There, in the third millennium BCE, the Hongshan culture produced jade plaques in the shapes of various birds and animals. These jade-working traditions seem to have influenced artisans of the later Shang dynasty (see photograph, page 51). The most recent discoveries, made in the early 1990s at two different late Western Zhou sites, included elaborate necklaces and belts made of jade pendants, all found undisturbed on the corpses in the tombs (see also photograph, page 93).

ABOVE Some of the earliest jade pieces ever discovered (see main text, left) include round disks with a hole in the middle, known as *bi* disks, that are believed to represent heaven. The jade *bi* shown here is from a later period, the Han dynasty (202 BCE–220 CE). Also discovered were rectangular blocks with a tubular hole known as *cong*, thought to represent the Earth. The uniqueness of both the *bi* and the *cong*, and the mystery of their precise functions, make it impossible to accurately translate either term.

CRAFTS OF THE POTTER

ABOVE **This exquisite headrest with painted ducks is from the Tang dynasty (618–907 CE), a period that saw some of the most significant advances in ceramic production in ancient Chinese history.**

The ceramic tradition in China surpasses even that of jade in terms of duration, stretching from the sixth millennium BCE down to modern times. Indeed, in terms of sheer output, no other media, artistic or otherwise, could compete with the number of ceramic artifacts made in China over the millennia.

While archaeological discoveries in recent decades have caused a wholesale rethinking of the relationships among cultures during China's neolithic period, it is still the case that the country's earliest pottery can be broadly divided into two types—red painted ware usually termed "Yangshao," and black "Longshan" ware. Yangshao pottery has been found in sites stretching from Gansu in the west to central Henan in China's central plain, and from the early fifth millennium through to the late third millennium BCE. Shaped by hand, with flat bottoms, it was fired at around 1,832 degrees Fahrenheit (1,000 degrees Celsius). Many of the pieces were decorated with painted designs: some were simple whorls, others were more or less realistic depictions of birds and especially fish, with a few examples of human faces and forms.

Longshan pottery, on the other hand, reflects a completely different cultural tradition. It was found primarily in eastern China, first—in the late fourth millennium BCE—in Shandong, and then later also in areas extending west into the central plain. Wheel-thrown with exceptionally thin vessel walls (sometimes described as eggshell thin), and with components that included legs and handles, the vessels were subjected to a controlled firing that resulted in their distinctive dense black, uniform surface. It was once believed that these two pottery traditions reflected a fundamental cultural divide between western and eastern China, but most people would now probably agree that they reflect only two among many tendencies in ancient Chinese culture.

The ceramic creations of almost all of ancient China's historical periods are notable and distinctive in one form or another. For example, as early as the Shang and Western Zhou periods, glazed bowls were being fired at high temperatures approaching those of porcelain (2,462 degrees Fahrenheit; 1,350 degrees Celsius). And the *mingqi* or "spirit utensil" grave offerings of some 1,000 years later provide a three-dimensional representation of many aspects of Han life. But it is the art of the Tang dynasty that probably constitutes the most important developments in the later history of Chinese ceramics. The *sancai* or "three-color" glazed bowls, and especially figurines, also found in tombs, are surely among the most eye-catching examples of this art. Brown, blue, green, red, and yellow lead glazes were applied to different parts of the figure; the glazes were then allowed to run together naturally in places, producing an almost tie-dyed effect.

Perhaps even more stunning, however, is the Yue ware of the southern Jiangsu and Zhejiang provinces. Drawing on a long tradition of pottery-making in the area, Tang potters there began producing a glorious crackled green celadon that would eventually set the standard for porcelain across all of East Asia. From this time on, the kilns of this region would be at the very heart of a booming ceramics industry.

BELOW A distinctive scroll design and soft, wonderfully muted earth tones adorn this cocoon-shaped jar dating from the 2nd century BCE.

METAL OF RITUAL

ABOVE **Bronze ritual vessel in the shape of an owl, from the Shang dynasty (13th to 12th century BCE). Bronze vessels were often used during the Shang dynasty to make offerings to ancestral spirits. Vessels came in various shapes and styles, but only a few took the form of animals or birds.**

There are many myths regarding the origins of metallurgy in China, but most of them revolve around the figure of Yu the Great, the tamer of China's floodwaters. After draining the water from the land, he is supposed to have cast nine bronze cauldrons to represent the nine regions of China (see page 31). Archaeology has presented some evidence for this myth. The earliest bronze ritual vessels found to date come from a site called Yanshi Erlitou, just outside of Luoyang, Henan. The culture associated with this site is more or less coterminous—both in terms of chronology and territory—with the way early texts describe the Xia dynasty (see page 34), the dynasty said to have been founded by Yu.

Although metallurgy surely originated in western Asia, and the notion of smelting ore into a liquid that could then be shaped into a solid metal was probably transmitted from there to China some time in the third millennium BCE. Once in China, it developed in a unique way, influenced in large part by the long indigenous pottery tradition. Whereas in the West, bronzes of any complexity were cast using a technique called lost-wax, in China bronze vessels were cast in a sectional ceramic assemblage. This method, known as piece-mold casting, began with the making of a pottery model of the vessel one wished to produce. Around this were placed two or, usually, more pieces of clay. Once the impressions of the model had been registered on the clay molds, they were taken off and fired. In order to dismantle them without losing any part of the model impression, the mold usually had to be symmetrical—this obviously had a great influence on the shapes in which Chinese bronzes could be produced.

Next, the clay of the model had to be scraped away to whatever thickness was desired for the final bronze vessel. The model then became the core of the mold assembly, into which it was replaced; it was held in place by small pieces of scrap bronze of the same thickness as the desired vessel. Finally, molten bronze would be poured into this assemblage. Once it had cooled, the mold and any exposed pieces of the core would be removed. Although this method is far more complicated than the lost-wax method of casting (and it was even more complicated when inscriptions were cast into the vessel), it had the very considerable advantage of affording access to the inside of the mold. While any desired intaglio (or engraved pattern) designs could be executed on the model, with this method, the bronze caster could also incise directly into the mold, creating relief design on the surface of the bronze. For this reason, it is the ornamentation on Chinese bronzes (the mature expression of which is seen on vessels from the Shang dynasty), rather than their shapes, that is recognized as being so unique in the world.

FANTASTIC BEASTS

Elite tombs from the Warring States period state of Chu usually contain wooden
statues of fantastic animals, often with protruding tongues, deer antlers, and claws.
They were often placed behind the coffin chamber to protect the deceased in the
afterlife. By the Han dynasty, these figurines had begun to be carved in stone and
had moved outside to guard the tomb entrances. They reached their artistic apogee
in the imaginary combinations of animals of the Six Dynasties and Tang periods. The
fabulous creatures shown here are all from the Tang era and depict winged spirits
(left and right), a dragon (above), and two fearsome earth-spirit figurines (opposite).

ETERNAL MUSIC AND POETRY

Shortly after the turn of the first millennium BCE, a new type of bronze bell was imported from southern China into the north-China heartland of the Zhou dynasty. This bell, arranged in sets of different sizes (and, thus, timbres) gave rise to the development of a more melodic style of music. Its introduction seems to have had a profound and wide-ranging effect on many aspects of Zhou life.

The most direct effect was doubtless on poetry, which was then sung, and sometimes danced, to the accompaniment of music. China's earliest poetry, a collection of 305 poems in the *Classic of Poetry*, includes temple liturgies, court hymns singing of heroes past and present, and "airs" that are variously understood as simple love songs or as political allegories. This poetry, sung to a staccato four-beat line, has had a great influence on all forms of Chinese written expression, both in terms of the symbolism that was derived from it and of the phrasing and formulation of the prose (which, like this poetry, tended to be written in complementary couplets of four-character phrases).

Confucius (551–479 BCE) is believed to have edited the *Classic of Poetry* and thus to have fixed its form for all time. Ironically, around this period, new musical instruments begin to appear in the archaeological inventory—including, prominently, wind and string instruments. These gave

LEFT A 6th-century CE Northern Wei-dynasty female musician playing a *qin* or zither. According to several notable ancient Chinese thinkers and philosophers, including Confucius (551–479 BCE), music was essential to the maintenance of order and harmony in society. The art of music was, in fact, held in such high regard that Emperor Wu of the Han dynasty (see pages 62–63) established an Imperial Office of Music. Placing great importance on the accurate tuning of instruments, the ancient Chinese were the first to develop the science of acoustics.

rise to a type of chamber music that was probably more lilting and languorous, at least as seen from the poetry that was sung to it. The meter of this new verse became much longer, with a breathing caesura built into every line. The length of the line allowed for greater description; what we would term adjectives and adverbs now became very prominent. Although Confucians railed against this "modern" music, and although formal court music continued to make use of the traditional percussion instruments and the shorter, more staccato meter, the most renowned poets of the next several centuries, from Qu Yuan (ca. 300 BCE) in the Warring States period, to Sima Xiangru (179–117 BCE) at the beginning of the Han dynasty, all exploited the free rhythms of the new music.

The collapse of the Han dynasty in the decades before and after the turn of the third century CE saw the rise of a new style of regulated verse that would set the standard for all Chinese poetry thereafter until the twentieth century. From the beginning of this period until the high Tang was the age of the great individual lyric poets, from Cao Pi (187–226), who would reign (220–226) as Emperor Wen of the newly established Wei dynasty (220–264); to Ruan Ji (210–263) and Ji Kang (223–262), two of the "Seven Sages of the Bamboo Grove" (see page 67); to Tao Qian (or Tao Yuanming, 365–427) and Xie Lingyun (385–433), who sang of the natural beauty they found in southern China; to the great Li Bai (701–762) and Du Fu (712–770) in the Tang dynasty. It was Du Fu who perhaps penned the epitaph for ancient China. Upon his return to the Tang capital Chang'an after it had been devastated in the course of the An Lushan (died 757) rebellion from 755 to 763 (see page 69), he wrote a poem entitled *Spring Gaze*, the first line of which reads: "The kingdom is destroyed; the mountains and rivers are here."

ABOVE **A wide variety of wind and string instruments, chimes, drums, and bells was used in ancient Chinese music. The pottery bell shown here is from the Eastern Zhou dynasty.**

PHILOSOPHICAL TRADITIONS

All of China's earliest writings, the *Classic of Poetry* as well as the *Classic of Documents* and the *Classic of Changes*, and no doubt even the oracle-bone inscriptions of the Shang dynasty, portray a universe in which humankind and nature are inextricably linked. This worldview is the foundation for China's correlative cosmology—the notion that actions in the human realm have corresponding effects (but not necessarily reactions) in the natural world, and vice versa.

In one influential account of the development of Chinese philosophy, this original union of heaven, Earth, and humans was sundered—probably about the fourth century BCE, in the middle of China's Warring States period. This apparently provoked an intellectual crisis that gave rise to the full flowering of Chinese philosophical expression, known as the "Hundred Schools" of thought (see page 55). Confucians, Daoists, Mohists, Legalists, Agriculturalists, and Militarists, as well as Logicians, and no doubt countless others whose thoughts have disappeared without a trace—all, over the next century or two, debated and wrote about the nature of life and the proper way (in Chinese, *dao*, meaning road or way) to lead it.

Two political/intellectual developments of the third and second centuries BCE would set the terms of most of China's non-Buddhist philosophy throughout the remainder of the ancient period. Part of the triumph of the Qin unification of China was the establishment of a system of correspondences, by which all elements in the world were correlated once again. This system, known as the "Five Motions" or "Five Phases," governed not only theories of natural science, but was also adapted to all aspects of philosophical discourse. A century later, with the recognition of Confucianism as the state philosophy during the reign of Emperor Wu (reigned 141–87 BCE) of the following Han dynasty, and especially with his establishment of an imperial

academy with the classics as the sole curriculum, much philosophical argumentation took the form of learned commentaries on the classics. The pervasiveness of the commentarial tradition can be seen in the importance that the founding emperors of the Tang dynasty attached to a project called the "Correct Meaning of the Five Classics." The project was designed to synthesize the commentaries written in the preceding four hundred years of political disunion, thereby reuniting the intellectual traditions of the north and south, just as the Tang had reunited them politically.

BELOW Philosophers, writers, and poets have long been enticed by the enchanting beauty and sacred vitality of sites such as Mount Huang, which serve as a powerful focus for their contemplation of the nature and mystery of existence.

CULINARY ARTS

BELOW An earthenware fishmonger from the Eastern Han dynasty (25–220 CE). Already depicted on Yangshao pottery from the fifth millennium BCE, fish came to symbolize fertility and prosperity. It was, of course, also a staple part of the diet, not only in coastal areas but also inland. Later texts describe how seafood was transported throughout the country packed in urine, a natural preservative.

The art of cooking was so popular in ancient China that it often served as a metaphor for philosophers. Both Confucius (551–479 BCE) and Laozi (sixth century BCE) advised that the state should be governed as one would cook a fish—delicately and with as little fuss as possible. Nor is the subject of drink overlooked: poems in the *Classic of Poetry* describe drunken guests at banquets after having made offerings to their ancestors; and, like many poets both before and after him, the great Li Bai (701–762 CE) seems to have found creative inspiration in a glass of wine.

Other authors collected recipes. In *Essentials for the Common People* (*Qi min yao shu*), completed in 540 CE, Jia Sixie included 280 recipes, ranging from fermentation techniques, to roasts and stews, noodles and breads. There is even a detailed description of how to make cottage cheese. As in all good cookbooks, Jia's recipes record the ingredients, amounts, preparation, and how to present the finished dish. It is clear that many of his recipes were taken from earlier cookbooks. Some of them are quoted as coming from a *Classic of Food* (*Shi jing*). Bibliographies of the time do record such a title (cookbooks were listed under medical literature), although it is listed as having been written by a northerner, while Jia was a southerner. At a time of disunion in China, it seems doubtful that books traveled so quickly—*Classic of Food* is therefore likely to have been a generic title used by a number of cookbooks.

One of the most recent discoveries of bamboo-strip documents has revealed an even earlier cookbook. In 1999, the tomb of Wu Yang (died 162 BCE) was excavated at Huxishan, in Yuanling, Hunan. Among the texts in the tomb were some 300 bamboo strips with at least 155 different recipes, 148 of which seem to be elaborate meat preparations. Although part of the text was damaged and the complete version has not yet been published, one recipe for slabs of suckling pig is available. It

LEFT A late Tang-dynasty wall-painting from Dunhuang, Gansu, depicting a butcher shop. The butcher is shown chopping an unidentifiable meat, while a dead ram lies beneath his chopping block. A famous story from the Daoist text *Zhuangzi* tells of a butcher so accomplished in his art that his cleaver never became dull—a metaphor for doing things in accord with the *Dao* or the "Way."

includes instructions for the butchering of the pig, removing its hair, cleaning its skin, and multiple stages of steaming and boiling, before a final boiling in a fresh sweet beef broth with wine, salt, meat-sauce liquid, ginger, and magnolia bark. The text indicates that horse, lamb, or venison can be prepared in the same way.

Although there are similarities between Wu Yang's cookbook and that of Jia Sixie seven centuries later, China's cuisine underwent many changes throughout that period. The demographic shift southwards that had begun in the fourth century CE familiarized China's elites with a host of new crops, including rice. The subsequent reunification of China under the Sui dynasty and the construction of the Grand Canal finally allowed for the transportation of this supremely important staple to the north, transforming the way people ate. In the next centuries, during the Tang dynasty, the introduction of another new southern crop—tea—was to have a profound influence on China's drinking habits, as well as its cultural traditions.

HEALING AND MEDICINE

BELOW This silk chart of 168 BCE from Mawangdui, illustrating 44 different gymnastics postures, is believed to be related to later meditation poses that were intended to visualize and concentrate spirits at desired points in the human body.

Medicine in China was inextricably bound up with all aspects of the traditional Chinese worldview. In popular conceptions, the human body was perceived as a microcosm of the universe: the celestial bodies all had their counterparts in the physical organs, as did mountains and waterways, plants and animals. Just as there were sometimes disruptions in the normal functioning of the natural order, such as drought or floods, so too was the body susceptible to malfunction; the purpose of medicine was to restore the natural order.

The development of the notion of the "Five Motions" or "Five Phases" in natural philosophy (see page 112) was readily adapted to this view of the body. Each of the

phases or processes was considered to correspond to an emotional, visceral, or physiological function of the body. Outside the body, the five processes corresponded to different foods and drugs. This gave rise to a very elaborate *materia medica* that could be used to treat imbalances of any of the processes. In the early second century BCE, a manuscript called the *Fifty-two Prescriptions*, discovered in 1973 at Mawangdui, in Changsha, Hunan, describes how to combine more than 200 different ingredients to treat specific diseases.

At the same time as the system of Five Phases was reaching its mature development, a new, in some ways simpler, conception of the body came to be adopted by elite doctors. They saw the body as being composed of three major constituents: *jing*, or concentrated fluids; *qi*, vapor or breath; and *shen*, or spirits. Each of these constituents played a vital role in maintaining a vigorous and healthy body.

While *jing* and *shen* might be regarded as the most refined constituents of the body, it was *qi* that was thought to pervade all aspects of it, circulating within it along various specified vessels or channels. The flow of *qi* through these channels gave rise to perhaps the most unique aspect of traditional Chinese medicine— acupuncture—the insertion of needles into specific points on the skin to influence the course the *qi* takes through the body.

LACQUERWARE

Lacquerware is almost unique to China (and to the rest of East and Southeast Asia, whence it spread from China), and is thus the artistic medium perhaps least well appreciated in the West. Its name refers to the lac tree (*Rhus vernicifera*), and especially to its sap, and should be strictly distinguished from shellac, which derives from the gummy deposit the *Tachardia lacca* insect leaves on trees. Although today the lac tree grows only in southern China (as well as in Thailand, Korea, and Japan), the *Classic of Poetry* includes references to it in states along the Yellow river, and the "Tribute of Yu" chapter of the *Classic of Documents* suggests that it was found in parts of central China. When the sap of the lac tree is exposed to oxygen, it polymerizes—in other words, it forms molecules of much higher weight, and therefore behaves like a plastic. Impervious to water, and also highly resistant to heat and acids, it was very much prized as a protective covering for a range of materials, especially wood and leather, and was used in many different ways—not only, for example, as a coating for all manner of food and wine utensils but also for items such as armor and coffins.

Numerous coats of lacquer were applied usually to a wooden base, although sometimes hemp was used as well, each coat being allowed to dry thoroughly before the next was added. The classical ritual texts state that in the Zhou dynasty when a king first acceded to power, his coffin would be made of the finest wood. Then every year thereafter, a coating of lacquer would be added to it; in the case of a king such as King Ping (reigned 770–720 BCE), the

RIGHT AND BELOW Two examples of lacquerware, both from the time of the Western Han dynasty (202 BCE–9 CE), but nevertheless revealing distinct differences in color and patterning—an indication of the wonderful diversity of styles that was produced during the period. The traditional art of lacquerware is unique to China and has continued, uninterrupted, for thousands of years.

first king of the Eastern Zhou period who reigned for fifty years, his coffin must have been very well protected indeed. Coffins from later elite tombs, such as that of Lord Yi of Zeng (died 433 BCE), do feature lacquer coatings that have preserved them almost perfectly, despite the waterlogged environment.

Lacquer itself is clear, but from an early period, Chinese artisans added pigments to it so that it could also be used for decorative purposes. Red and black were the two most common pigments, with a convention for eating and drinking utensils to be black on the outside and red on the inside. However, other colors could also be used, and applied in such a way that lacquer could well be said to be the medium for China's earliest paintings. The coffin of Lady Dai (died ca. 165 BCE) at Mawangdui, for instance, features swirling clouds upon which various fantastic demons ride while engaging in battle with each other. Other decorative forms could be carved directly into the lacquer, which when hard could be cut or engraved in the same way as wood or stone.

SECRETS OF SILK

Although not ranked as one of China's four great inventions (the compass, gunpowder, paper, and printing), silk was perhaps its greatest contribution to world civilization. Spun from the filaments of cocoons of the domestic silkworm (*Bombyx mori* is the finest), silk is a fiber of extraordinary properties: it has phenomenal tensile strength and is so elastic that it can be stretched by up to twenty percent of its length before it will tear; and it has the greatest affinity to dye of any natural fiber. Silk clothing keeps one cool in summer but warm in winter. It is no wonder that people throughout the ancient world sought to understand the secret of its production and, failing that, paid great sums to obtain it.

The invention of silk spinning in China is credited to Xiling Shi, wife of the Yellow Emperor, in the third millennium BCE. And indeed, there is artifactual evidence of loom-woven silk from no later than the middle of the second millennium. The cultivation of silkworms and the production of silk were probably not much different then than in later times. Silk production is a labor intensive and very delicate process, which begins with the cultivated mulberry tree and the silkworms. Unlike the wild mulberry tree, which produces many berries but few leaves, the domestic mulberry produces few berries but many leaves. This is essential because it is the leaves that are fed to the silkworms. Over 1 ton (about 1,000 kilograms) of leaves is needed to rear just 1 ounce (28 grams) or so of newly hatched silkworms, which produce around 6 pounds (2.7 kilograms) of reeled silk. The worms feed for about thirty-five days, for the last few days consuming twenty times their body weight in leaves. When they reach their mature size of approximately 2 inches (5 centimeters) in length, they spend another five days spinning their cocoon, and then eight to ten days inside it.

Just before the chrysalis is due to exit, the cocoon is immersed in boiling water, killing the chrysalis and dissolving the sericin that binds the filaments; the timing of this last step is crucial because if the chrysalis is allowed to exit the cocoon, it secretes a liquid that ruins the spun filaments. With the cocoon still in the water, the filaments are caught on a comb and then reeled with a reeling machine.

By the Han dynasty, when trade along the Silk Road first thrived (see page 122), silk was manufactured on a grand scale. In 110 BCE, the office in charge of regulating silk prices had five million rolls of silk in storage. The Han government used silk as a commodity to buy peace among the peoples along its northwestern frontier. In 91 CE alone, the silk given to just the southern Xiongnu was valued at 100,900,000 pieces of currency, more than one percent of the state's gross national product.

LEFT Silk filaments were dyed almost every conceivable color using plant dyes and were then woven on looms. Designs came in many different forms, from flowing clouds to continuous geometric shapes to meandering floral motifs, as in the fine Tang-dynasty example (9th to 10th century CE) shown here. Such designs and motifs were used in Chinese art for centuries.

THE SILK ROAD

China's most famous road, the Silk Road, refers to a continuous chain of oasis towns that stretched from Chang'an (present-day Xi'an), the capital of both the Han and Tang dynasties, westward through the Gansu corridor, and then separated at Jiuquan and Dunhuang and skirted either side of the Taklamakan desert—Anxi or Hami, Turfan, Kucha, and Aksa, along the Tian Shan or Heavenly Mountains to the north, and Charkhlik, Niya, Khotan, and Yarkand, along the Kunlun Mountains to the south—before rejoining at Kashgar, and then continuing through Kokand, Tashkent, Samarkand and Bakhara, and finally reaching the Syr-Darya and Amu-Darya. The view of a section of the ancient route shown here (right) is of the riverbed to the northwest of Kucha, Xinjiang province, near the Tian Shan Mountains. This arid, salt-encrusted landscape is transformed in the summer months, when water flows down from the mountains.

Although people and goods had been moving along these routes since time immemorial, it was during China's most flourishing periods—the Han and Tang dynasties—that the most thriving trade was conducted. Caravans were like moving cities; in one raid in 135 CE, bandits are reported to have seized more than 1,000 cartloads driven by Chinese merchants from Hebei. Much of the trade was driven by the desire of western peoples, including those of the Roman Empire, to obtain Chinese silk. During the Han dynasty, the trade was largely one-sided, with the Han government using silk to buy political influence in Central Asia. Under the Tang, on the other hand, luxury goods and people flowed into Chang'an, making it then almost surely the most cosmopolitan city in the world.

A STORY-TELLING TRADITION

Chinese literature has always given pride of place to poetry and then to historical narrative; drama and fiction did not come into their own until well after the ancient period. In fact, their origins are much debated. A genre of short stories, often concerned with records of strange and supernatural events, burst on the scene early in the Six Dynasties period (222–589), and continued to develop throughout the Tang dynasty (618–907). Some scholars believe that this was inspired by the coming of Buddhism to China. Buddhist *sutras* are often filled with great detail of the divine transformations of *buddhas* and *bodhisattvas* ("enlightenment beings"), and Buddhist missionaries also tended to teach this new religion by way of fabulous stories of reward and retribution. Many examples of these "transformation texts" were discovered early in the twentieth century at the Buddhist cave complex of Dunhuang (see page 70). Other scholars counter that China's early traditions of historical narrative and philosophical writing in the form of short parables could easily have stimulated the "records of the strange" that appeared in the fourth century of the common era.

RIGHT **An illustration from the *Vimalakirtinirdesha sutra*, early 10th century CE, ink and color on paper. After Kumarajiva (344–413) first translated this classic of Mahayana Buddhism into Chinese in about 406 CE, its humorous and dramatic narratives made it a favorite of Chinese readers, Buddhist and non-Buddhist alike. It is probably the case that such Buddhist *sutras* had a profound influence on the development of Chinese fiction.**

There is doubtless some truth in both these accounts of the origins of Chinese fictional story-telling, but archaeological discoveries suggest another stimulus as well. In 1986, in a tomb at Fangmatan in Gansu province, an early example of a ghost story was unearthed. The story is presented as an official report on a court case that took place in 300 BCE. A man named Dan had committed suicide after stabbing a neighbor. Three years later, the village headman petitioned the gods to let Dan return to life, arguing that he had not yet been fated to die. The gods sent a white dog to dig up Dan's tomb; once released, he came back to life, still bearing the scar where he had slit his throat.

This story was not unusual at the time it was written. Indeed, another tomb, in Henan, closed in 299 BCE but reopened by tomb robbers in 279 CE, contained a collection of similar tales. When the contents of the tomb were transported to the capital and edited, they were an instant success, fascinating a wide circle of scholars and writers. The sudden popularity of the ghost story in this period was almost certainly stimulated by this discovery, giving new life to a long forgotten literary tradition.

PAINTING AND CALLIGRAPHY

If one takes account of the designs and inscriptions on all the ceramics, bronzes, lacquers, and stone carvings in China, then the history of the related arts of painting and calligraphy may be seen as being very old. Even if the definition is restricted to brushwork on silk (and, later, paper), the famous Chu Silk Manuscript from the Warring States period (480–222 BCE) would have to count as an early example of both painting and calligraphy. Also found in the same tomb as this manuscript was the earliest known silk funeral banner, a precursor to the more famous example from Mawangdui (see photograph, page 97). These attest to what must have been a vigorous tradition of painting. Unfortunately, no actual paintings survive from the period, and no individual artist or calligrapher was mentioned in literary sources.

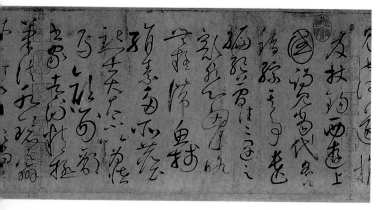

ABOVE **Detail from the autobiography of the monk Huai Su, famed for his cursive style of calligraphy. Tang dynasty, 777 CE.**

It is only with the Six Dynasties period (222–589) that we can put names to painting and calligraphy. Wang Xizhi (307–365), known to posterity as the "Sacred Calligrapher," has left not only examples of his penmanship, but also a treatise in which he describes his philosophy of writing—each individual character must reveal the psychology of the scribe. Psychological expression was also paramount to Wang's younger contemporary, Gu Kaizhi (ca. 344–406). Gu rebelled against the tendency of the time to focus on costume and symbolic icons, insisting that the face should be the center of attention. He emphasized the "bone structure" of the painting ("bone" referring to the line of the brush, seeking by way of it to arrive at the inner truth of the subject). He argued that in painting historical pictures, the purpose was not to present a realist scene but rather to display feelings and values.

Landscape painting, the genre most strongly associated with Chinese art, did not really come into its own until the glory years of the Tang dynasty. Wang Wei (699–759), the famous poet, was also an accomplished landscape artist, the first embodiment of the scholar-painter. Even more influential in terms of the great landscape tradition of late imperial China was Wu Daozi (flourished 740–760). Using only black ink, he held that the quickness of the brushwork revealed the clarity of the image in the mind of the artist. When commissioned to paint a handscroll showing thousands of miles of scenery, he completed the work in a single day.

LEFT *Admonitions of the Instructress to the Court Ladies* is a 9th- or 10th-century copy of a handscroll, ink and color painting on silk, by Gu Kaizhi (ca. 344–406). The scroll illustrates aphorisms contained in the literary work, *Record of Things Far and Wide* by Zhang Hua (230–300). Gu Kaizhi believed that painting should express values and emotions. He held that a scene with two or more people in it was preferable to one with a lone figure, because it allowed for the expression of a relationship.

SCULPTURE

Until relatively recently, it was generally thought that prior to the coming of Buddhism to China in roughly the first century of the common era, China had no indigenous tradition of sculpture. There was evidence of bronzes in the shapes of fantastic creatures; of twelve gigantic statues—commissioned by the First Emperor of Qin (reigned 221–210 BCE)—that were cast using bronze melted down from weapons collected throughout the empire; and of a statue at the tomb of Huo Qu-bing (died 117 BCE) showing a horse trampling a Xiongnu warrior. But there was little or no indication of attempts to model the human body in the round. In this context, the discovery of the 7,000 life-size terracotta soldiers, each individually differentiated, in the pit near the tomb of the First Emperor was even more astounding than it would otherwise have been (see pages 48, 49). The years since that great discovery have brought much more evidence of a native tradition of sculpting the human form—from the giant bronze figures found at Sanxingdui (see pages 18, 23), to the small jade figurines in the Shang tomb of Fu Hao, to the thousands of statuettes, both male and female, found near the tomb of Emperor Jing of the Han (reigned 157–141 BCE). This tradition shows how Chinese artisans transformed Indian Buddhist sculpture when it was introduced into China toward the end of the Han dynasty.

Chinese Buddhist sculpture, and by implication Daoist sculpture as well, is generally characterized by a head-on perspective, with considerable emphasis on the head and little or no suggestion of body movement—although the latter did evolve over time. Some of the earliest Buddhist sculpture preserved today was created during the Northern Wei dynasty (386–534). Ruled by the Toba or Tabgatch, a people of mixed Turkic and Mongol stock, the state sponsored the building of massive figures of the Buddha and *bodhisattvas* ("enlightenment beings") in caves, first at

Yungang near their first capital at Pingcheng (present-day Datong, Shanxi), and then, after moving the capital to the more central Luoyang (in Henan), at Longmen. The free-standing statues, as opposed to earlier examples carved into the walls of caves and temples, testify to a religious function: they were designed to be circum-ambulated by the faithful, who, at the same time, would view the scenes from the Buddhist *sutras* that adorned the walls of the surrounding cave.

When China was reunited under the Sui dynasty (581–618), Emperor Wen (reigned 581–605) was also a great patron of Buddhism. It is said that during his reign one and a half million old images of the Buddha were repaired, and one hundred thousand new ones made. The sculptures of the period are distinctive. They feature the earliest extant free-standing statues, more or less life size. They are considerably less mannered than their predecessors, with a flowing line to the body and a hint of irony in the facial features. These trends continued into the Tang dynasty, though with new influences. In 645, when Xuan-zang returned from his sixteen-year pilgrimage to India, he brought with him seven statues of the Buddha; these apparently stimulated a new phase of sculpture-making. By the time of the female emperor Wu Zetian (reigned 684–705), statues of *bodhisattvas* can only be described as voluptuous, revealing a pronounced femininity.

RIGHT A Sui-dynasty limestone head of a Buddhist *bodhisattva* with a serene facial expression. The figure depicted may be Guanyin, the embodiment of compassion. Under Sui leadership, Buddhism acquired powerful patronage and a new sculptural style evolved in which figurative and bodily realism combined with religiously inspired expressions of transcendent calm and tranquillity.

—129—

ARCHITECTURE

Just as, prior to the introduction of Buddhism to China, the human form was not prominently displayed in statuary, so too was there concealment in both residential life and architecture. From the earliest evidence we have through to the end of the ancient period (and well into the modern period, for that matter), Chinese buildings were set, for privacy and protection, behind high walls. Indeed, urban life in general was hidden from view and conducted within a series of nested walls. Cities were almost by definition surrounded by walls (the English words "city" and "wall" are often both translated by just one word in Chinese, *cheng*).

Within the city walls, districts might also be divided by walls, within which individual residences were demarcated by yet another wall. And within the exterior walls of the largest residences, and especially of government palaces, there were still further recesses, designed to exclude both commoners and enemies: public life was conducted in a forecourt between the exterior gate and a central pavilion, while private life took place around a back court that was situated behind the pavilion (or pavilions). The remains of what Chinese archaeologists believe may have been the royal palace of the Xia dynasty have been excavated at Yanshi Erlitou, just outside

LEFT AND ABOVE **An elaborately detailed Eastern Han pottery model, 2nd century BCE, of a five-story grain silo excavated from Henan province. The silo is set within an exterior wall, which encloses a central courtyard. The three roofs on the upper stories reveal well the cantilevered roof style that is characteristic of traditional Chinese architecture, although the height of this model is unusual for its early period.**

Luoyang, Henan; they show these features already in the middle of the second millennium BCE. The Forbidden City in Beijing can be seen as the full flowering of this building style.

The structure of Chinese buildings in general has tended to be quite conservative. It featured a rectangular foundation of rammed earth which raised the floor of the building above ground level. Into this foundation—and set back from its perimeter—was set a series of wooden pillars that bore the weight of the roof. The roof was also constructed of wooden eaves, supporting a superstructure which from early times was covered with ceramic tiles. The nature of the roof required that buildings be wider than they were deep, and that the roof be relatively low. In the mature architecture of the Tang dynasty (618–907), the height of the roof was set at one sixth of the depth of the building. It was the one feature of the building that might be seen from outside the external wall of the compound, and was therefore often brightly colored and decorated with auspicious animals and symbols.

The one notable exception to this architecture of concealment was the Buddhist pagoda, doubtless the most conspicuous humanmade feature of China's late antiquity. Developing from the *stupa* mounds which were used in India as repositories for relics, the pagoda quickly took on a distinctive look in China. Often built of brick rather than wood (the only previous use of brick in China had been in tomb construction from the Han period, and it is possible that the pagoda's reliquary function influenced this choice of material), the Chinese pagoda came to be built up in multiple stories. The almost 200-foot (61-meter) high Great Goose Pagoda, erected in Xi'an in 652 CE (see pages 132–133), is perhaps the most famous but by no means the tallest of the thousands of pagodas dotting Tang China's countryside.

GREAT GOOSE PAGODA

The Da Yan Ta or Great Goose Pagoda (right) is the
oldest extant multi-storied brick structure in China.
Located in the Ci'en Si or Temple of Mercy in the
Tang-dynasty capital of Chang'an (present-day Xi'an,
Shaanxi), it was erected in 652 CE to commemorate the
return to China of Xuanzang, the temple's abbot, from
his sixteen-year pilgrimage to India in search of
Buddhist scriptures.

The original structure of the building comprised
five stories rising to a height of 177 feet (54 m). Within
a half century, during the reign of the Empress Wu
Zetian (684–705), this original structure was
demolished and replaced by a new one—according to
the same design, but now with six stories, built on a
square foundation, 137 feet (42 m) each side and more
than 16 feet (5 m) high. A seventh story was added in
the middle of the eighth century, bringing the pagoda
to a height of 196 feet (60 m). After this time, the
pagoda's appearance seems not to have been changed.

An interior staircase rises to the very top of the
structure, and the climbing of it has been a notable
motif in Chinese literature since no later than 752
when Du Fu (712–770), one of ancient China's greatest
poets, celebrated his visit to the Great Goose Pagoda
with a poem. It serves almost as an epitaph for ancient
China, reading in part:

> "The high standard straddles the blue sky,
> The cold wind at no time ceases.
> I myself am not of carefree heart;
> Climbing here I turn over our hundred woes. ...
>
> Alas, drinking at the Jasper Pool,
> The sun sets into the Kunlun peaks.
> The yellow swan departs without stopping.
> Where does its mournful cry hit?
> I watch the geese following the sun,
> Each plotting to get a morsel of grain."

GLOSSARY

acupuncture The ancient Chinese practice of inserting needles into the skin to alleviate pain or cure disease.

archaeology The study of artifacts from human history and prehistory.

astrology The study of how the movements of celestial bodies affect the human condition.

bodhisattva In the Buddhist religion, a being that is able to achieve enlightenment.

Bronze age The prehistoric period during which bronze was primarily used to fashion weapons and tools.

Buddhism An Asian religion founded in the fifth century BCE in India that focuses on the roots of human suffering and enlightenment.

calligraphy The art of handwriting.

Daoism A Chinese philosophy based on the writings of Lao-Tzu.

dynasty A multigenerational ruling family.

Hunan A province in eastern-central China.

jade A green stone used widely in Chinese jewelry.

lacquerware Ceramics that have a lacquer coating.

metaphysics Describing that which is beyond the laws of traditional physics.

monk A religious follower who has sacrificed something for his beliefs.

mummification The process of preserving the dead by embalming and wrapping in cloth.

mural A painting that is created directly on the wall on which it is displayed.

neolithic Relating to the latter part of the Stone Age.

pagoda A Buddhist temple.

pictograph The art of using pictures or symbols to denote words.

reincarnation The belief that living creatures come back as other living creatures after death.

Silk route A route that linked central China with the eastern Mediterranean Sea.

sutra A rule or lesson.

FOR MORE INFORMATION

The British Museum

Ancient China

38 Russell Square

London, WC1B 3QQ

England

Web site: http://www.ancientchina.co.uk

One of the most respected museums in the world, the British Museum's Ancient China exhibit features Chinese history, artifacts, and writings.

China Institute

125 East 65th Street

New York, NY 10065

(212) 744-8181

Web site: http://www.chinainstitute.org

Founded in 1926, the China Institute educates visitors about the art, history, and culture of China.

Chinese American Museum

El Pueblo de Los Angeles

125 Paseo de la Plaza, Suite 400

Los Angeles, CA 90012

(213) 485-8567

Web site: http://www.camla.org

The Chinese American Museum, located in Southern California, chronicles the Chinese-American experience and history of the region.

Web Sites

Due to the changing nature of Internet links, Rosen Publishing has developed an online list of Web sites related to the subject of this book. The site is updated regularly. Please use this link to access the list:

http://www.rosenlinks.com/civ/china

FOR FURTHER READING

Berger, Patricia Ann., et al. *Tomb Treasures from China: The Buried Art of Ancient Xi'an*. San Francisco, CA: Asian Art Museum of San Francisco, 1994.

Birrell, Anne. *Chinese Mythology: An Introduction*. Baltimore, MD: John Hopkins University Press, 1993.

Chang, Kwang-chih. *The Archaeology of Ancient China*. 4th ed. New Haven, CT: Yale University Press, 1986.

Falkenhausen, Lothar von. *Suspended Music: Chime-Bells in the Culture of Bronze Age China*. Berkeley, CA: University of California Press, 1993.

Fong, Wen. (ed.) *The Great Bronze Age of China: An Exhibition from the People's Republic of China*. New York, NY: Metropolitan Museum of Art, 1980.

Graham, A.C. *Disputers of the Tao: Philosophical Argument in Ancient China*. La Salle, IL: Open Court Press, 1989.

Granet, Marcel. *La pensée chinoise*. 1934. (Reprinted Paris: Albin Michel, 1968.)

Harper, Donald. *Early Chinese Medical Literature: The Mawangdui Medical Manuscripts*. London, England: Kegan Paul, 1997.

Keightley, David N. *Sources of Shang History: The Oracle-Bone Inscriptions of Bronze Age China*. Berkeley, CA: University of California Press, 1978.

Legge, James. *The Chinese Classics*. 5 Vols. London, England: 1865–72; Oxford, England: 1893–94; (Reprinted Hong Kong: Hong Kong University Press, 1960.)

Lewis, Mark Edward. *Writing and Authority in Early China*. Albany, NY: SUNY Press, 1999.

Little, Steven. (ed., with Shawn Eichman.) *Taoism and the Arts of China*. Chicago, IL: Art Institute of Chicago, 2000.

Loewe, Michael. *Divination, Mythology and Monarchy in Han China*. Cambridge, England: Cambridge University Press, 1994.

Loewe, Michael. (ed.) *Early Chinese Texts: A Bibliographical Guide*. Berkeley, CA: The Society for the Study of Early China and the Institute of East Asian Studies, University of California, 1993.

Loewe, Michael, and Shaughnessy, Edward L. (eds.) *The Cambridge History of Ancient China: From the Beginnings of Civilization to 221 B.C.*. New York, NY: Cambridge University Press, 1998.

McMullen, David. *State and Scholars in T'ang China*. Cambridge, England: Cambridge University Press, 1988.

Needham, Joseph. *Science and Civilization in China*. 8 Vols. Cambridge, England: Cambridge University Press, 1955-.

Pirazzoli-t'Serstevens, Michèle. *The Han Dynasty*. New York, NY: Rizzoli, 1982.

Rawson, Jessica, ed. *Mysteries of Ancient China: New Discoveries from the Early Dynasties*. London, England: British Museum Press, 1996.

Scarpari, Maurizio. *Splendours of Ancient China*. London, England: Thames and Hudson, 2000.

Schafer, Edward H. *The Golden Peaches of Samarkand: A Study of T'ang Exotics*. Berkeley, CA: University of California Press, 1967.

Shaughnessy, Edward L. (ed.) *New Sources of Early Chinese History: An Introduction to the Reading of Inscriptions and Manuscripts*. Berkeley, CA: The Society for the Study of Early China and the Institute of East Asian Studies, University of California, 1997.

Shaughnessy, Edward L. (ed.) *China: Land of the Heavenly Dragon*. London, England, and New York, NY: Duncan Baird Publishers and Oxford University Press, 2000.

Sickman, Laurance, and Soper, Alexander. *The Art and Architecture of China*. Harmondsworth, England: Penguin Books, 1968.

Stein, Aurel. *On Ancient Central-Asian Tracks*. Chicago, IL: University of Chicago Press, 1964.

Steinhardt, Nancy R.S. *Chinese Traditional Architecture*. New York, NY: China Institute, 1984.

Tsien, Tsuen-hsuin. *Written on Bamboo and Silk: The Beginnings of Chinese Books and Inscriptions*. 2nd rev. ed. Chicago, IL: University of Chicago Press, 2004.

Twitchett, Denis. (ed.) *The Cambridge History of China*. Vol. 3, Part 1: Sui and T'ang China, 589–906. Cambridge: Cambridge University Press, 1979.

Twitchett, Denis, and Loewe, Michael. (ed.) *The Cambridge History of China. Vol. 1: The Ch'in and Han Empires (221 B.C.–A.D. 220)*. Cambridge, England: Cambridge University Press, 1986.

Watson, William. *The Arts of China to A.D. 900*. New Haven, CT: Yale University Press, 1995.

Whitfield, Roderick, and Farrar, Anne. *Caves of the Thousand Buddhas: Chinese Art from the Silk Route*. London, England: The British Museum, 1990.

Wu, Hung. *Monumentality in Early Chinese Art and Architecture*. Stanford, CT: Stanford University Press, 1995.

Yang, Xiaoneng. (ed.) *The Golden Age of Chinese Archaeology: Celebrated Discoveries from the People's Republic of China*. New Haven, CT: Yale University Press, 1999.

Yang, Xiaoneng. (ed.) *New Perspectives on China's Past: Chinese Archaeology in the Twentieth Century*. 2 Vols. New Haven, CT: Yale University Press, 2004.

Zürcher, Erik. *The Buddhist Conquest of China: The Spread and Adaptation of Buddhism in Early Medieval China*. 2 Vols. Leiden, Netherlands: Brill, 1959.

INDEX

ABOUT THE AUTHOR

Edward L. Shaughnessy is Creel Professor of Early China in the Department of East Asian Languages and Civilizations, University of Chicago. His many publications include *Sources of Western Zhou History: Inscribed Bronze Vessels*, *I Ching: The Classic of Changes*, *Before Confucius: Studies in the Creation of Chinese Classics*, and *The Cambridge History of Ancient China*. He is also the General Editor of *China: Reference Classics*.

PICTURE CREDITS

The publisher would like to thank the following people, museums and photographic libraries for permission to reproduce their material. Every care has been taken to trace copyright holders. However, if we have omitted anyone we apologize and will, if informed, make corrections to any future edition.

Key:

l	left	t	top
r	right	b	bottom
AKG	AKG-images, London		
BL	British Library, London		
BM	British Museum, London		
Christie's	Christie's Images, London		
CRP	Cultural Relics Publishing House, Beijing		
RHPL	Robert Harding Picture Library, London		
ROM	Royal Ontario Museum		
WFA	Werner Forman Archive, London		

Page 4 CRP/Hunan Provincial Museum, Changsha; **5** Ray Main/Mainstream/Institute of Archaeology, Beijing; **7** Christie's; **8** Corbis/ROM/Richard Swiecki; **9** AKG/Fufeng County Museum/Laurent Lecat; **10** WFA/Provincial Museum, Xian; **11** BL; **12** BL; **13** Corbis/ROM/Brian Boyle; **15** Christie's; **16** Christie's; **17** CRP/National Museum of Chinese History, Beijing; **20** Rex Features, London; **21** Christie's; **22** Corbis/ROM; **23** CRP/Institute of Archaeology and Cultural Relics Bureau, Sichuan; **24** Getty/Stone/Keren Su; **25** WFA; **27 & 28** BM; **30** Getty/Stone/Keren Su; **31** BM; **32–33** Corbis/Tiziana and Gianni Baldizzone; **34** CRP/Institute of Archaeology, Beijing; **37** BM; **38** Getty/Image Bank/Joseph Van Os; **41** CRP/Sichuan Provincial Museum, Chengdu; **42** National Museum of Chinese History, Beijing; **44** BL; **45** WFA; **46–47** WFA; **48 & 49** Corbis/Keren Su/Mausoleum of Emperor Qin, Xian, Lintong county, Shaanxi; **50 & 51** Christie's; **52–53** Christie's; **54 l** BM; **54 r** Christie's; **55** WFA; **57** Art Archive/Jan Vinchon Numismatist, Paris/Dagli Orti; **59** Index/Summerfield; **60–61** Corbis/Keren Su; **62 & 63** Christie's; **65** RHPL/Robin Hanbury-Tenison; **66** Christie's; **67** Christie's; **69** WFA/Idemitsu Museum of Arts, Tokyo; **70–71** CRP; **72–73** Christie's; **74** Réunion des Musées Nationaux/Musée Guimet, Paris/Thierry Ollivier; **75 & 76** Christie's; **77** RHPL/Robin Hanbury-Tenison; **78** WFA/National Palace Museum, Taipei; **81** Corbis/Lowell Georgia; **84** Corbis/Asian Art & Archaeology, Inc.; **85** RHPL/Nigel Blythe; **88** RHPL/Robin Hanbury-Tenison; **87** Ray Main/Mainstream/Cultural Relics Bureau, Xindu county, Sichuan; **89** BM; **90** Christie's; **91** Corbis/Asian Art & Archaeology, Inc; **93** CRP; **94** Index/ Summerfield; **97** Institute of Cultural Relics, Beijing; **98–99** Corbis/Lowell Georgia; **100** CRP/Hunan Provincial Museum, Changsha; **101** Christie's; **100** BM; **101 & 102** Christie's; **103** Corbis/ROM; **106** Corbis/Burstein Collection; **107 t** Corbis/ROM; **107 b** Corbis/Asian Art & Archaeology, Inc; **109** Corbis/Christie's; **110** Art Archive/Musée Guimet, Paris/Dagli Orti; **111** Seattle Art Museum, Eugene Fuller Memorial Collection/Paul Macapia; **113** Magnum Photos/Stuart Franklin; **114** Bridgeman Art Library/Oriental Bronzes Ltd, London; **115** Reproduced by permission of the Commercial Press (Hong Kong) Limited from the publication *The Complete Collection of Dunhuang Grottoes—Paintings of Folk Costumes*; **116** Joseph Needham Institute, Cambridge; **128 l & 118–119** Corbis/Asian Art & Archaeology, Inc.; **121** BM; **122–123** John Warburton-Lee Photography/Antonia Tozer; **124–125** BM; **126** WFA/National Palace Museum, Taipei; **127** BM; **129** Christie's; **130** Ray Main/Mainstream/Henan Provincial Museum, Zhengzhou; **132–133** Tropix/Veronica Birley.